Managing Complex Projects

A NEW MODEL

Managing Complex Projects

A NEW MODEL

KATHLEEN B. HASS, PMP

MANAGEMENTCONCEPTS

ΓΓΓ
MANAGEMENTCONCEPTS

8230 Leesburg Pike, Suite 800
Vienna, VA 22182
(703) 790-9595
Fax: (703) 790-1371
www.managementconcepts.com

Printed in the United States of America

Library of Congress Cataloging-in-Publication Data

Hass, Kathleen B.
    Managing complex projects : a new model / Kathleen B. Hass.
        p. cm.
    ISBN 978-1-56726-233-9
1. Project management. I. Title.
    HD69.P75H3757 2009
    658.4'04—dc22

                                                                            2008027192

10   9   8   7   6   5   4   3   2   1

PRAISE FOR
Managing Complex Projects: A New Model

Kitty's book is refreshing, insightful, and on-target. This is a serious look at the challenges we face today in managing complexity on projects. Though it is serious, it is a delight to read. Her research is impeccable, her sources current, and her ideas original. Managers who listen to her arguments and follow her advice will be at a great advantage in dealing with the 21st century's brave new world of complex project management.

J. DAVIDSON FRAME, PhD, PMP, PMI FELLOW
ACADEMIC DEAN, UNIVERSITY OF MANAGEMENT AND TECHNOLOGY
AUTHOR OF *THE NEW PROJECT MANAGEMENT: TOOLS FOR AN AGE OF RAPID CHANGE, COMPLEXITY, AND OTHER BUSINESS REALITIES*

"Using breakthrough thinking, Kitty unravels the mysteries of project complexity and offers a proven model to succeed in the chaotic marketplace. For those who are lost in a tangled web of challenged projects, this book not only offers a way out but a way to thrive. It is a welcome breath of fresh air and cure for the (common) complex project."

B. MICHAEL AUCOIN, D. ENGR., PE, PMP
PRESIDENT, LEADING EDGE MANAGEMENT, LLC
AUTHOR OF *RIGHT-BRAIN PROJECT MANAGEMENT: A COMPLEMENTARY APPROACH*

"Projects today operate in the midst of constantly changing business conditions and complex technologies. Combine that with things like distributed delivery and other complicating organizational factors—and project managers are faced with dramatically increasing complexity on their projects. Kitty's approach gives these managers a framework and tools to handle this increasing complexity that nicely supplement their formal project management training and work experience."

SANJIV AUGUSTINE
PRESIDENT, LITHESPEED
AUTHOR OF *MANAGING AGILE PROJECTS*

About the Author

Kathleen (Kitty) B. Hass is the Senior Practice Consultant for Management Concepts. She is a prominent presenter at industry conferences and is an author and lecturer in strategic project management and business analysis disciplines. Her expertise includes leading technology and software-intensive projects, building and leading strategic project teams, and conducting program management for large, complex engagements.

Kitty has more than 25 years of experience in project management and business analysis, including project portfolio management, business process reengineering, IT applications development and technology deployment, project management and business analysis training and mentoring, and requirements management. She has managed large, complex projects in the airline, telecommunications, retail, and manufacturing industries as well as in the U.S. federal government.

Kitty's consulting experience includes engagements with multiple federal agencies, including USDA, USGS, NARA, and an agency within the intelligence community, as well as industry engagements at Colorado Springs utilities, Toyota Financial Services, Toyota Motor Sales, the Salt Lake Organizing Committee for the 2002 Olympic Winter Games, and Hilti US Inc. Kitty is Director at Large for the International Institute of Business Analysis (IIBA®) and has served as a member of the IIBA® Business Analysis Body of Knowledge™ committee.

She holds a BA in business administration, summa cum laude, from Western Connecticut University.

To . . .

My brilliant husband, whose thinking permeates these pages

My amazing children, Patrick, Sally and Dave, Joey and Christy—
I love watching them soar

And my even more amazing grandchildren, Alec, C.J., Madeline, and Liam—
I can't wait to see them take wings

Contents

Foreword

The question often asked about project management is "why do so many projects fail?" Project management looks easy enough, and the concept of project management is quite simple: find a need, create a plan to meet that need, execute the plan, and you're done!

The first step, identifying the need, is often the most straightforward. This may be the requirement for a new product or service that will meet market demand, or it may reflect a need to increase effectiveness or efficiency to improve competitiveness. These are "what" is needed. "How" to meet the need, or the plan to achieve it, is a bit more of a challenge, and the execution of the plan can be excruciatingly difficult. Both these factors depend on the complexity of the project.

Business today is often complex and moves so rapidly that developing a solution to meet an organizational or market need (the plan) is equally, if not more, complex. Because of this complexity, the success rate for projects is abysmally low. According to the Standish Group, only about one-third of all IT projects are successfully completed as originally envisioned. Many are outright failures, are terminated before completion, or are never implemented even if they are completed because they fail to meet customer or user expectations. Why is this? Kitty Hass has zeroed in on the correct answer to deal with this problem of project complexity. The answer is to do the right projects to begin with, and then to do them in the right way based on their complexity.

First of all, are the right projects being selected to be done? Who decides which are the right projects? With the scarce resources available in any organization, and the amount and pace of change in business today, the demand is for increased acknowledgment—and acceptance—of responsibility by senior management for which projects are to be undertaken. The next question is, does management really know which are the right projects? The answer demands that senior management identify organizational goals, develop the strategies that will achieve those goals, and then choose the projects that will ensure that the organization will meet those strategies and achieve the goals. Kitty defines an approach for senior management to use after the right projects to conduct are identified.

Once the right projects are identified, the question of how they are to be done becomes critical; this is, as Kitty has found, a major problem in today's world of project management. In many cases traditional project management models don't work in the current business environment. As Kitty clearly shows, 21st century projects require new thinking and a new approach. She provides the insight for this approach to projects by treating them as complex adaptive systems that are themselves part of an even larger complex system, the global economy. To succeed, complex projects must follow an approach that involves complexity thinking, which she describes in terms of complexity theory. The result is a new *Project Complexity Model* that can be used as the framework for determining the approach needed to manage a project based on the level of complexity involved.

Kitty's *Project Complexity Model* provides a framework for diagnosing complexity on a wide variety of projects, ranging from small, independent, short projects, to medium size and medium complexity projects, through large, highly complex, longer projects. The model guides the project manager through a three-step process to ensure that (1) the appropriate project leader is assigned, (2) the appropriate project cycle is selected, and (3) the appropriate management style is chosen for the complexity dimensions involved. To guide the reader, detailed suggestions are provided for completing each of these steps to meet specific project needs.

Anyone—indeed, everyone—facing the challenging task of managing one of today's complex projects will find much in this book to aid them in their efforts to carry out successful projects.

Gerald M. Mulenburg, DBA
National Aeronautics and Space Administration

Preface

I have been working in the project environment for more than 25 years. During that time I have developed a keen understanding of the degree of difficulty involved in managing projects of any size. As projects get bigger and more complex, we tend to "do more of the same," applying ever greater degrees of rigor in the way of methods, reviews, and tests, resulting in higher costs but not necessarily returning value.

THE MOVEMENT HAS STARTED

It is now becoming clear that our conventional project management processes are inadequate for managing complex projects. Research is underway by the Project Management Institute and others to determine what makes projects complex and to learn how to manage project complexity. Many thought leaders in the field of project management are presenting alternative approaches for managing complex projects; many of these works are cited in this book.

So the movement has started. Unprecedented change is occurring all around us because of the global economy, the Internet, and the ubiquitous nature of information technology. Because projects are our means to execute strategies and react to changes in the marketplace, the capability to carry out project management effectively is no longer an option. If organizations are unable to execute projects, their very survival is likely to be at risk. Recognizing that the stakes are so high, we are beginning to redefine project success to be about delivering *business value* as opposed to simply delivering on time, on budget, and on scope. Yet, our ability to manage complex projects is immature and inadequate. We are now realizing that new approaches are desperately needed to manage complex projects in the ever-changing global economic environment.

INTRODUCING THE *PROJECT COMPLEXITY MODEL*

In this book we explore the nature of complexity theory as it applies to projects. We contend that complexity abounds in 21st century projects; that project teams are complex adaptive social systems nested within companies, which are in turn complex adaptive systems operating within the global economy (which is also a complex adaptive system); and that large-scale complex business solutions must be adaptive—easy to change as the business environment changes. Thus, our challenge is to learn how to employ complexity thinking as a complement to our conventional project management methods to manage 21st century projects.

This book presents a new model for project leadership teams to use to diagnose project complexity and to make decisions about how to plan and manage projects based on their complexity profile. Anyone challenged with filling a leadership role on a critical project will benefit from learning how to apply complexity thinking to make managerial decisions on projects.

It is no longer just about the project manager. Success depends on a combination of disciplines; therefore, complex projects must be led by a highly seasoned, multitalented senior team of strategic thinkers. The complex project leadership team should be made up of the best resources available— experienced project managers, business analysts, solution architects and developers, and a business visionary. The members of this project leadership team will collaboratively diagnose the dimensions of their project's complexity using the new *Project Complexity Model.* Armed with an in-depth understanding of the nature of the complexities they are dealing with, they will be equipped to make managerial decisions about how to reduce and manage those complexities. As project success improves, we will all benefit.

HOW THIS BOOK IS ORGANIZED

In the Introduction we explore the current state of project performance. We look at the extent of, and reasons for, unprecedented change in the business environment. We then consider the track record for project performance—which is quite alarming—and present the case for finding new ways to think about and manage complex projects. The book is then divided into four parts.

Part One defines and explores the nature of complexity theory and complex adaptive systems, and suggests how complexity science can be applied to projects. We compare and contrast conventional project management techniques with adaptive approaches that use complexity thinking. We then introduce our *Project Complexity Model* and offer guidance on how to use the model to help manage complex projects.

Part Two suggests using the *Project Complexity Model* to inform decisions about project resource assignments. We provide an overview of the competencies required to manage complex projects, discuss strategies for developing managers of complex projects, and make recommendations for applying complexity thinking to select leaders of complex projects.

Part Three suggests using the *Project Complexity Model* to make decisions about the appropriate project cycle to use. We discuss and recommend appropriate project cycles for independent, low-risk projects; for moderately complex projects; and for highly complex projects.

Part Four is the heart of the book. We turn our attention to the nature of complexity dimensions, probe the causes of the different aspects of complexity, and offer suggestions for dealing with each complexity dimension using the *Project Complexity Model*. We then analyze all the dimensions of complexity delineated in the model, including large, long-duration projects; projects with multiple dispersed, diverse project teams; urgent projects; projects with unclear business problems, opportunities, or solutions; projects with volatile, ambiguous requirements; highly visible, politically sensitive projects; projects involving large-scale cultural change; projects dependent on external factors and constraints; and projects involving unproven IT technology.

Managing complex projects is no simple matter. We hope our *Project Complexity Model* will shed some light and provide some helpful direction for you in your quest to manage the particular complexities of your project.

Kitty Hass
Castle Rock, Colorado

Acknowledgments

As this book goes to print, I am reliving my career in fast forward. My early career was with Unisys. I often say that you don't really know how good a company is until you leave it. Unisys was one of those great companies. I must acknowledge my first manager at Unisys, Russ Bonacci. As IT Director, Russ enabled me to reach out beyond our IT departmental responsibilities to seek training and experience beyond that which would help his group accomplish its goals. Russ truly enabled me to fly, into quality management, software capability improvement using the Software Engineering Institute's Capability Maturity Model, and even the model for performance excellence, the Baldrige National Quality Program. I have leveraged these broad competencies, knowledge, and experiences throughout the rest of my career. This experience taught me that excellence is acquired through continually assessing current capabilities and striving to raise the bar.

Contributors to this book are many, and some of them don't even know it. My colleagues at Management Concepts, John Kinser, Don Wessels, and Merleen Hilley, were kind enough to review and comment on the very first iteration of this book, which was in the form of a white paper. My engineering colleagues at the CIA, who must remain nameless, provided valuable insights into the world of complex engineering projects. My former manager, Cleve Pillifant, was not only inspirational but quite supportive in the birth of this volume. My partner in crime, Teidi Tucker, always props me up and offers words of encouragement.

In addition, many thought leaders in the field of complex project management have greatly influenced me; most of them are widely quoted in this book. First and foremost is Doug DeCarlo, author of *eXtreme Project Management: Using Leadership, Principles, and Tools to Deliver Value in the Face of Volatility*. Doug has made a lasting contribution to our ability to deliver value through projects in the face of uncertainty and volatility. Dr. Gerald Mulenburg offered words of encouragement and contributed to sections of the book describing complexity theory as it applies to projects. Michael Aucoin presented a revolutionary approach to looking at projects in *Right-Brain Project Management: A Complementary Approach*, as did Aaron J. Shenhar and Dov Dvir in their groundbreaking work, *Reinventing Project Management: The Diamond Approach to Successful Growth and Innovation*.

I would like to acknowledge the work of the editors, Myra Strauss and Lena Johnson, who polished the manuscript with great talent and consideration. In addition, Myra has been an extraordinary source of encouragement and support throughout. Management Concepts in general is a remarkable place to work—supportive, leading edge, and above all, concerned about its people. This I must attribute to our leader, Tom Dungan, and his leadership team.

Unprecedented Change in the Business Environment

"I think the 21st century will be the century of complexity."

—Professor Stephen W. Hawking, PhD, Physicist

On the brink of the 21st century, Jonathan Wilson, owner of Anabasis Consulting, which focuses on leadership, strategy, and complexity theory in the business context, set the stage for us. Wilson noted that change is happening faster than ever and is causing fundamental shifts in the business environment in which we plan and execute projects.

JONATHAN WILSON
Anabasis Consulting[1]

Forecasting based on measurement and control is losing its relevance as a tool for successful planning and organization management. In the new business climate an understanding of chaos and complexity theory will be the key to winning performance.

Just at the time that change has become the dominant theme of modern management, the nature of change itself is changing. It is happening not just more quickly, but faster than ever. It is happening in new ways with more turbulence, less predictability. The key cause of the changing of change in business is the acceleration of the flow of information and the exponential increase in the number of connections within and between organizations. "No man is an island" and no corporation can insulate itself any longer. There is continuous interplay and feedback between and within organizations happening faster and faster.

We see the effects of all this change on business processes, organizational structures, and business solutions. Business processes have become more complex than ever before, manifested in more interconnections, interdependencies, and interrelationships. Businesses today are rejecting traditional management structures to create complex organizational communities made up of alliances with strategic suppliers, networks of customers, and partnerships with key political groups, regulatory entities, and even competitors. Through these alliances, organizations are addressing the pressures of unprecedented change, global competition, time-to-market compression, rapidly changing technologies, and increasing complexity at every turn.

Twenty-first century projects deal with behaviors arising from the interdependence of users, technology, and context, which are often referred to as "wicked" problems.[2] Innovative products and business systems are significantly more complex than in the past; accordingly, the projects aimed at implementing 21st century solutions are more complex. In the business world, whole new industries are emerging, mergers and acquisitions are rampant, and existing industries are in the process of remaking themselves. All these fundamental transformations are in response to the rapidly changing global marketplace, mobilization, and urgent business needs.

TRACK RECORD FOR COMPLEX PROJECTS

Project management is the primary method worldwide for introducing change in a wide variety of industries—many of which have not yet mastered the discipline. Huge cost and schedule overruns are commonplace in large public works projects. Major, complex, unpredictable public works projects that have never been attempted before often result in mammoth cost overruns and schedule extensions of months if not years. Consider, for example, Boston's "Big Dig," the central artery/tunnel project, which began construction in 1991, ran into major problems, and was finally completed in December 2007. It was originally supposed to cost about $2.5 billion and is now up to over $14.6 billion.

The worlds of product development and IT are quickly merging, as so many consumer products depend on software to operate. Yet, software-intensive system development is one of the glaring examples where even the largest companies are still struggling to invest in project management to produce high-quality products that work out of the box. Is this situation the result of the complexity of the product or the complexity of software project management? John Kenagy, the CIO at Oregon Health & Science University, a medical college with a teaching hospital based in Portland, Oregon, suggests this underlying cause: "Historically, I don't think IT professionals and leaders have had the same regard and respect for project management as a unique IT discipline as they do for technical positions such as database administrators and programmers. The thought has traditionally been, 'We're all working on projects, so everybody should have project management skills.'"[3]

An abundance of research conducted over the last 15 years has revealed the rather dismal record of project performance, particularly for software projects. The Standish Group, which specializes in IT value research, has been conducting studies on IT project performance and publishing the results in *The CHAOS Report* since 1994. The CHAOS research, considered to be *the* groundbreaking study of IT project performance, has been continually updated since its first publication and is widely referenced in the project management and IT industries.

The original 1994 Standish Group research study exposed the overwhelming failure of IT application development projects and estimated that American companies and government agencies spend $80 billion–$145 billion per year on failed and canceled software-intensive projects. The latest research was completed in 2006 and released in 2007 (Figure I-1). The Standish Group's *2007 First Quarter Research Report* exposed the continuing challenges of IT projects across industries: Only 35 percent of projects are successful (deliver on time, on budget, and with full scope of features and functions), 46 percent are challenged (the project is completed and the new solution is operational, but it was late and over budget, with reduced features and functions), and 19 percent fail (do not deliver anything of value).[4]

For their groundbreaking book advocating a new approach to managing complex projects, *Reinventing Project Management: The Diamond Approach to Successful Growth and Innovation*, authors Aaron Shenhar and Dov Dvir collected data for 15 years on more than 600 projects in the business, government, and nonprofit sectors in various countries. They found that 85 percent of projects failed to meet time and budget goals, with an average overrun of 70 percent in time and 60 percent in budget. The primary reason for these failures was that ". . . executives as well as project teams failed to appreciate up front the extent of uncertainty and complexity involved (or failed to communicate this extent to each other) and failed to adapt their management style to the situation."[5]

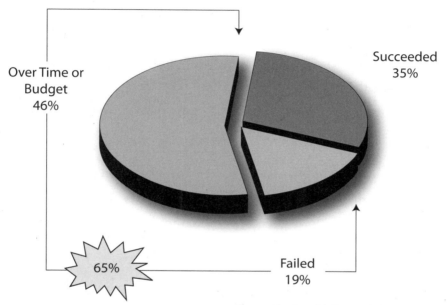

IT Projects in the United States, 2006 Survey

Over Time or Budget 46%

Succeeded 35%

65%

Failed 19%

Source: The Standish Group, 2006 Chaos Report

FIGURE I-1. The Standish Group 2006 Chaos Report

For a public sector source of comparable information, we look to the Office of Management and Budget (OMB), the federal government agency that evaluates the effectiveness of federal programs, policies, and procedures; assesses competing funding demands among agencies; sets funding priorities; and approves funds for major capital projects. A 2003 OMB study stated that "771 projects included in the fiscal 2004 budget—with a total cost of $20.9 billion—are currently at risk. . . ." OMB concluded that the high cost of failure is unsustainable.[6]

Finally, let us look to the United Kingdom for another view of project success for complex initiatives. A study on the state of IT project management in the United Kingdom conducted by Oxford University and *British Computer Weekly* revealed that a mere 16 percent of IT projects were considered successful.[7] Similarly, a survey conducted and published by *British Computer Weekly* found that only three out of the more than 500 development projects evaluated met the survey's criteria for success.[8] What is the cost of failed and challenged IT projects? Although admittedly difficult to quantify, a 2003 analysis estimated a phenomenal US$150 billion per year attributed to IT project failures in the United States with a further US$140 billion in the European Union.[9]

The implications are obvious: We need to determine how to improve our ability to manage complex and critical projects. Over the last two decades, many efforts have been undertaken to drive improvements, with some success.

EFFORTS TO IMPROVE PROJECT PERFORMANCE

*"We know why projects fail, we know how to prevent their failure—
so why do they continue to fail?"*

—MARTIN COBB, COBB'S PARADOX,
TREASURY BOARD OF CANADA SECRETARIAT, OTTAWA, CANADA

Since the early 1990s, project success rates have improved across the board and the frequency of cost and schedule overruns has been declining. Again referencing the latest Standish Group research:[10]

The new CHAOS report . . . reveals that 35 percent of software projects started in 2006 can be categorized as successful, meaning they were completed on time, on budget and met user requirements. This is a marked improvement from the first, groundbreaking report in 1994 that labeled only 16.2 percent of projects as successful; that report galvanized an industry of development tools vendors selling everything from requirements management solutions to modeling tools and turned software architecture into a cottage industry.

Further, the 2006 study shows that only 19 percent of projects begun were outright failures, compared with 31.1 percent in 1994. The 2006 report is the sixth published by The Standish Group, and Chairman Jim Johnson said that with the exception of a lapse in 2004, "we've seen consistently better software projects. ·

Several initiatives undertaken to address the project performance crisis have, without a doubt, contributed to the increase in project success rates:

➤ The Federal IT Project Manager Initiative was chartered to raise the capability and maturity of project management for major IT initiatives in the federal government.[11] A 2004 General Accounting Office (GAO, now called the Government Accountability Office) report determined that software-intensive weapon acquisitions are increasingly critical, and current practices are insufficient to meet the challenge.[12] The term "software crisis" was used to focus attention on the improvements needed for successful management of software-intensive projects.

➤ The Clinger-Cohen Act was enacted in 1996 to institute private-sector IT management best practices in federal agencies. The law requires the largest agencies to create a chief information officer (CIO) position to provide strategic insight into how IT could help mold the business processes used to deliver public services.

➤ The U.S. Department of Defense (DoD) established the Software Engineering Institute at Carnegie Mellon University to promote mature, quality-based project management practices.

➤ The Software Productivity Consortium, later renamed the Systems and Software Consortium, Inc. (SSCI) (www.software.org), was formed in the late 1980s to provide industry and government a resource for insight, advice, and tools that could help them address the complex and dynamic world of software and systems development.

➤ Sophisticated educational programs were created, such as the Defense Systems Management College on the Management of Software Acquisition and the graduate software engineering program at George Mason University.

➤ Advanced standards, such as DoD acquisition standards 2167 and 2168, were developed.

➤ The DoD Software Technology for Adaptable, Reliable Systems (STARS) program was established to ". . . accelerate, coordinate, and disseminate the results of R&D in software technology, bridging the gulf between future and current software technology states of practice, and meeting the need for an improved software state-of-practice."[13]

➤ The IT Governance Institute (ITGI™) (www.itgi.org) was formed in 1998 to advance international thinking and standards in directing and controlling IT groups to ensure that IT supports business goals, optimizes business investment in IT, and appropriately manages IT-related risks and opportunities. Also from ITGI™, the Control Objectives for Information and Related Technology (COBIT®) provides a comprehensive framework for the management and delivery of high-quality IT-based services.

➤ The Project Management Institute (PMI), long acknowledged as a pioneer in the field of project management, has a truly global membership of more than 260,000 professionals in 125 countries.

➤ The International Institute for Business Analysis (IIBA) is the leading worldwide professional association that develops and maintains standards for the practice of business analysis and for the certification of practitioners.

➤ New project management methods have emerged to more effectively manage dynamic projects that involve a high degree of uncertainty and urgency (e.g., agile project management). These methods delay decision-making as long as possible and rely heavily on iteration and innovation.

➤ IT Service Management (ITSM) is a philosophy that focuses on IT as a service provider as opposed to a technology provider. Proponents of ITSM believe we should describe information technology as business technology, with IT results measured in terms of business benefits.

➤ PMI's Research Program and industry thought leaders have been focusing on understanding the nature of complex projects and applying complexity thinking to manage the dimensions of project complexity.

Table I-1 depicts the resolution of 30,000 applications projects in large, medium, and small cross-industry U.S. companies tested by the Standish Group from 1994 to 2006.[14]

Year	Successful Projects	Failed Projects	Challenged Projects
2006	35%	19%	46%
2004	29%	18%	53%
2000	28%	23%	49%
1998	26%	28%	44%
1996	27%	40%	33%
1994	16%	31%	53%

TABLE I-1. Standish Group Project Resolution History (1994–2004)

Clearly there has been steady improvement in IT project performance. The reasons for the overall improvement include the following: (1) the average cost of a project had been downsized more than half by 2001; (2) better skilled project managers have been recruited for critical IT projects; and (3) better methods and tools to manage changes have been introduced. In addition, the Standish Group continually recommends minimizing project scope, reducing project resources, and downsizing timelines to improve project success.[15] Standish predicts that the number of critical projects will double each year; therefore, we must continue to work vigilantly to improve project performance, paying particular attention to the elements it calls the *Recipe for Project Success: The CHAOS Ten*, which are listed here in priority order.

Recipe for Project Success The CHAOS Ten[16]

1. Executive support
2. User involvement
3. Experienced project managers
4. Clear business objectives
5. Minimized scope
6. Standard software infrastructure

> 7. Firm basic requirements
> 8. Formal methodology
> 9. Reliable estimates
> 10. Other: small milestones, proper planning, competent staff, and ownership

The management approaches we recommend in Part IV of this book to improve complex project management draw heavily from the Standish Group's *Recipe for Project Success*.

IT'S ABOUT SURVIVAL

In an interview with Diann Daniel of CIO.com, Rudy Puryear, who heads IT for Bain & Company, a leading global business and strategy firm, offers insights into the consequences of our inability to manage complex change efforts.

RUDY PURYEAR
Bain & Company[17]

If you look back at Fortune 500 companies over the last couple of decades, a third ended up in bankruptcy, got acquired, or otherwise became integrated into another company. About another third had to fundamentally change their core strategy in order to be successful. Only 28 percent experienced no significant change, compared to the period from 1985 to 1994, when 51 percent of companies were stable. And the survival rate is likely to continue to decrease in the next decade because of the pace of change, because of the difficulty of change. The problem is that a lot of organizations have built unnecessary complexity into their business, and this complexity is beginning to act like reinforced concrete. It's a barrier to change.

To manage this unprecedented change and increase the numbers of successful projects, organizations need to be good at a number of very difficult business practices: (1) establishing business strategies and goals, (2) identifying new business opportunities, (3) using IT as a strategic asset, (4) determining the most valuable solutions to business problems, (5) selecting, prioritizing, and funding the most valuable major change initiatives, and (6) executing flawlessly to meet business needs and achieve strategic goals as quickly as possible. The major change initiatives will likely include:

➤ Business process improvement or reengineering ventures to replace complex, inefficient, and outmoded legacy business processes and technologies

➤ Initiatives to transform information from a utility for running the business to a competitive asset

➤ Significant change programs to tune the organizational structure, capabilities, and competencies as the business model changes, including organizational restructuring, down- or right-sizing, staff acquisition or retooling, establishing/relocating business operations, outsourcing selected operations, and mergers and acquisitions

➤ Programs to launch new lines of business, which will require new business processes, organizations, and technologies to support the new operations.

21st CENTURY PROJECTS

Virtually all organizations are investing in large-scale transformation of one kind or another. Contemporary projects are about adding value to the organization through implementing breakthrough ideas, optimizing business processes, and using IT as a competitive advantage. As we have seen, these initiatives are often spawned by mergers or acquisitions, new strategies, global competition, or the emergence of new technologies—all of which occur with a sense of great urgency. The projects carried out to implement these very difficult and multifaceted business changes are enormously complex.

Other initiatives are launched to implement new or reengineered business systems to drive waste out of business operations. Most of these projects are complex by virtue of the accompanying organizational restructurings, new partnerships, cultural transformation, downsizing or right-sizing, and enabling IT systems. Those that involve introducing new lines of business and new ways of doing business (e.g., e-business) require groundbreaking commercial practices.

In addition to these business-driven changes, IT organizations are transforming themselves, striving to become less complex, more service-oriented, and better aligned with the organization's core business. In the best organizations, IT has matured from focusing on stand-alone, specialized applications to fulfilling business needs aimed at achieving strategic goals and increasing profitability. In the 21st century, project teams are no longer dealing with IT projects in isolation, but within the overarching process of business transformation; the reach of change extends to all areas of the organization and beyond to customers, suppliers, and business partners—making the complexity of projects formidable.

Various dimensions of project complexity are likely to be present on large-scale change projects. Projects today comprise large, multilayered, geographically dispersed, and multicultural teams. Projects are urgent, yet they are too long in duration to be free from changing business needs. Projects often have a far-reaching but perhaps ill-defined and uncompromising scope. They frequently have aggressive schedules and inflexible budgets. All too often, projects have ambiguous, unstable, and poorly understood requirements.

The very nature of projects today and their strategic importance to the organization make them highly visible, politically charged, and riddled with conflicting expectations. Large-scale organizational change involves external constraints and dependencies, cultural sensitivity, and often unproven technology. Managing complex business projects requires a new kind of knowledge, skill, and ability—and a much stronger focus on the *business* versus the *technology*.

To reap the rewards of significant, large-scale change initiatives designed not only to keep businesses in the game but also to make or keep them major competitive players, we must find new ways to manage large, complex projects. We are beginning to realize that because such complex projects involve unpredictable interrelationships and interdependencies, they require a much more flexible and adaptive approach to project management and an understanding of complexity science. This book explores how the principles of complexity thinking can be used to find new, creative ways to think about and manage 21st century projects.

> Businesses today are attempting to react to—and preempt—the unprecedented level of change that is taking place as a result of the growing role of technology, the Internet, and the global marketplace. For organizations to thrive, indeed to survive, in the global economy, we must find ways to dramatically improve the performance of large-scale projects. Applying the concepts of complexity theory can complement conventional project management approaches and enable us to adapt to the unrelenting change that we ignore at our own peril.

NOTES

1. Jonathan Wilson, "No Plans for the Future," *Measuring Business Excellence,* vol. 3, no. 3 (1999). Online at http://www.trojanmice.com/index.htm (accessed January 2008).

2. Linda J. Vandergriff, "Complex Venture Acquisition," *Complexity Conference White Paper* (2006), 1.

3. Carol Hildebrand, "CIOs Make Project Management Skills a Priority," *SearchCIO.com* (January 24, 2005). Online at http://searchcio.techtarget.com/news/article/0,289142,sid182_gci1047064,00.html (accessed March 2008).

4. The Standish Group International, Inc., *2007 First Quarter Research Report,* (2006–2007).

5. Aaron Shenhar and Dov Dvir, *Reinventing Project Management: The Diamond Approach to Successful Growth and Innovation* (Boston: Harvard Business School Press, 2007), 5–7.

6. Office of Management and Budget, "Federal IT Project Management Initiative," (March 2003). Online at http://www.ocio.usda.gov/p_mgnt/doc/CIO_Council_Guidance.ppt#416,3, Federal IT Project Manager Initiative Action Plan (accessed May 2008).

7. Chris Sauer and Christine Cuthbertson, "Hitting Targets: The State of Project Management in the UK," *Computer Weekly.* Online at http://www.computerweekly.com/Articles/Article.aspx?liArticleID=198320&PrinterFriendly=true (accessed May 2008).

8. Andrew Taylor, "IT Projects Sink or Swim," *British Computer Society Review* (2001).

9. Darren Dalcher and Audley Genus, "Avoiding IS/IT Implementation Failure. Technology Analysis and Strategic Management," *TASM,* vol. 15, no. 4 (December 2003) 403–407.

10. David Rubinstein, "Standish Group Report: There's Less Development Chaos Today," *The Standish Group International, Inc.* (March 1, 2007), Online at http://www.sdtimes.com/article/story-20070301-01.html (accessed January 2008).

11. Office of Management and Budget, "Federal IT Project Management Initiative," (March 2003). Online at http://www.ocio.usda.gov/p_mgnt/doc/CIO_Council_Guidance.ppt# (accessed May 2008).

12. U.S. Government Accountability Office, "Defense Acquisitions: Stronger Management Practices Are Needed to Improve DOD's Software-Intensive Weapon Acquisitions," *Report to the Committee on Armed Services* (March 2004). Online at www.gao.gov/new.items/d04393.pdf (accessed January 2008).

13. Samuel T. Redwine, Jr., and Sarah H. Nash. "Need and Rationale for the Software Technology for Adaptable Reliable Systems (STARS) Program," ADA185665, Institute for Defense Analyses, Alexandria, Virginia. Abstract online at http://stinet.dtic.mil/oai/oai?verb=getRecord&metadataPrefix=html&identifier=ADA185665 (accessed May 2008).

14. The Standish Group International, Inc., "Extreme CHAOS," (2001). Online at http://www.smallfootprint.com/Portals/0/StandishGroupExtremeChaos2001.pdf (accessed January 2008).

15. Ibid.

16. Ibid.

17. Diann Daniel, "Complex IT Will Kill Your Business," *CIO online magazine* (July 27, 2007). Online at http://www.cio.com/article/print/126350 (accessed January 2008).

PART I

Complexity Thinking in the World of Business

In this part, we introduce complexity theory, the nature of complex adaptive systems, and their relevance to the world of business. We then present the case for applying complexity thinking to managing complex projects, building high-performing project teams, and selecting the appropriate management approach.

In Chapter 1 we briefly define complexity theory and consider the nature of complex adaptive systems. We then explore the notion of businesses and project teams as examples of complex adaptive systems.

In Chapter 2 we examine conventional project management approaches and consider whether they are sufficient for dealing with complex projects. We then present an adaptive approach to managing complex projects.

In Chapter 3 we introduce our *Project Complexity Model*. We explore when and how to use the model, focusing on the steps involved in applying complexity thinking to projects.

CHAPTER 1
Complexity Thinking

"I am convinced that the nations and people who master the new sciences of complexity will become the economic, cultural, and political superpowers of the next century."

—HEINZ PAGELS, PHYSICIST

D r. Gerry Gingrich, instructor at the Information Resources Management College, National Defense University, states: "Military thinkers, politicians, scientists, and corporate executives are all looking for ways to understand the dynamics of global change and to prepare for the 21st century. Many are looking to the new science of complexity for answers. The science of complexity, however, does not yield answers, at least not in the sense that we have typically sought to describe our world and predict its events since the beginning of the Scientific Revolution. What it does yield is a new way of thinking about the world."[1]

Complexity is one of those words that is difficult to define. Some say *complexity* is the opposite of *simplicity*; others say *complicated* is the opposite of *simple* while *complex* is the opposite of *independent.* A complex structure is said to use interwoven components that introduce mutual dependencies and produce more than the sum of their parts. In today's business systems, this is the difference between myriad connecting "stovepipes" and an effective set of "integrated" solutions.[2]

A complex system can also be described as one in which many different components interact in multiple ways.[3] In the context of a design that is difficult to understand or implement, complexity is the quality of being intricate and compounded.[4] When project managers characterize a project as complex, they usually mean the project is ". . . challenging to manage because of size, complicated interactions, or uncertainties. Often, anxiety goes hand in hand with complexity."[5]

Complex systems and complexity theory have captured the attention of scientists in the fields of anthropology, physics, biology, ecology, economics, political science, psychology, native studies, sociology, finance, and management. Since business organizations as well as project teams are complex systems, the science of complexity theory offers a way to understand and work with the complex nature of organizations and projects. Because complex systems are largely unpredictable, thinking about business systems as complex requires a paradigm shift from long-established business models based on control theory, which is essentially an attempt to manipulate the inputs to a system to obtain a desired effect on the output of the system.[6]

Complexity scientists are careful to differentiate between *complicated* and *complex. Complicated* is considered to have input and output flows and straightforward cause and effect (as in machines), where the pieces can be well understood in isolation and the whole can be reassembled from the parts; one problem can bring the system down, since complicated systems do not adapt.[7] *Complex*, in contrast, is adaptive (as in ecosystems), with cycles, interrelationships, interdependencies, nested systems within systems, and multiple feedback loops. Examples of complex systems include weather systems, the Internet, the U.S. power grid, highways, supply chains, information transfer within organizations, business systems, and business organizations themselves. According to Julio Ottino, professor at the R.R. McCormick School of Engineering and Applied Sciences at Northwestern University, "The hallmarks of these complex systems are adaptation, self-organization and emergence—no one designed the web or metabolic processes within a cell."[8]

COMPLEX SYSTEMS AND COMPLEXITY THEORY

Scientists originally thought the world to be linear, explained by simple cause-and-effect relationships. They theorized that if we could break down natural systems into their component parts, we could not only understand them but also learn how to predict and control them. Gradually, however, complexity theory emerged.

Complexity theory had its beginning in the 1980s at a think tank known as the Santa Fe Institute. Researchers ranging from graduate students to Nobel laureates formulated the theory that the application of ideas like complexity, adaptation, and turmoil at the edge of chaos can begin to explain ". . . the spontaneous, self-organizing dynamics of the world in a way that no one ever has before—with potential for immense impact on the conduct of economics, business, and even politics. They believe they are forging the first rigorous alternative to the kind of linear, reductionist thinking that has dominated science since the time of Newton—and that has now gone about as far as it can go in addressing the problems of the modern world."[9]

Complexity theory is based on relationships, emergence, patterns, and iterations. It maintains that the universe is full of systems (e.g., weather systems, immune systems, social systems) that are complex and are constantly adapting to their environment; hence the term *complex adaptive systems.*[10] Creativity manifests itself in spontaneous emergence, which is at the center of complexity thinking. Emergence is the result of the intricate interplay of dynamics, forces, and energies. Creativity emerges in systems that are constantly evolving, reorganizing, or dissolving into chaos. The genius of complexity thinking is that it nourishes and masters creativity, never trying to lock it into systems, subsystems, or parts.[11]

Complexity theory states that systems exist on a spectrum ranging from *equilibrium* to *chaos*. Equilibrium results in paralysis and death; chaos results in an inability to function. The most productive state to be in is at the *edge of chaos,* where maximum diversity and creativity lead to new possibilities[12] (Figure 1-1).

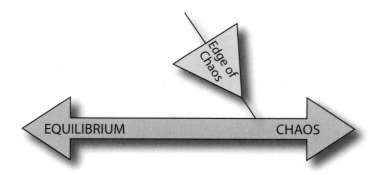

FIGURE 1-1. The Edge of Chaos, the Most Productive State

COMPLEX ADAPTIVE SYSTEMS

Complex adaptive systems are a specific type of complex system. These systems are *complex* in that they are diverse and comprise multiple interconnected elements; they are *adaptive* in that they have the capacity to change and learn from experience. The term "complex adaptive system" was coined at the Santa Fe Institute. In his essay, *A Brief Description of Complex Adaptive Systems and Complexity Theory,*[13] Peter Fryer describes the most important properties of complex adaptive systems:

➤ *Emergence.* Rather than being planned or controlled, the agents in the system interact in apparently random ways. From all these interactions, patterns emerge that inform the behavior of the agents within the system and the behavior of the system itself.

➤ *Co-evolution.* All systems exist within their own environment and they are also part of that environment. Therefore, as their environment changes, they need to change to ensure best fit.

➤ *Sub-optimal.* A complex adaptive system does not have to be perfect to thrive within its environment. It only has to be slightly better than its competitors; any energy used on being better than that is wasted energy.

➤ *Requisite variety.* The greater the variety within the system, the stronger it is. In fact, ambiguity and paradox abound in complex adaptive systems, which use contradictions to create new possibilities to co-evolve with their environment.

➤ *Connectivity.* The ways in which the agents in a system connect and relate to one another are critical to the survival of the system, because it is from these connections that the patterns are formed and the feedback is disseminated.

➤ *Simple rules.* Complex adaptive systems are not complicated. The emerging patterns may have a rich variety, but the rules governing the functioning of the system are quite simple.

➤ *Iteration.* Small changes in the initial conditions of the system can have significant effects after they have passed through the emergence-feedback loop a few times (often referred to as the *butterfly effect*).

➤ *Self-organizing.* There is no hierarchy of command and control in a complex adaptive system. Rather than planning or managing, there is a constant reorganizing to find the best fit with the environment.

➤ *Edge of chaos.* Complexity theory is not the same as chaos theory, which derives from mathematics. But chaos does have a place in complexity theory in that systems exist on a spectrum ranging from equilibrium to chaos.

➤ *Nested systems.* Most systems are nested within other systems, and many systems are made up of smaller systems.

BUSINESSES AND PROJECT TEAMS AS COMPLEX ADAPTIVE SYSTEMS

Complex adaptive systems are all around us: ant colonies, weather systems, the immune system, the brain, the stock market, business systems, and any group of people who are working toward similar goals, such as political parties, communities, businesses, and yes, *project teams*. The principles of emergence and self-organization are relevant in all these systems. Complex adaptive systems are a model for thinking about the world around us—but not a model for predicting what will happen.

Businesses are complex adaptive systems nested within a larger complex adaptive system, the global economy. Just as complex adaptive systems in nature fluctuate among the states of equilibrium, edge of chaos, and even chaos depending on their environment, so will a company fluctuate among these states. A business may at times operate in chaos, particularly when old ways of doing things need to be abandoned and new ways need to be found to explore and experiment with a variety of alternatives in an innovative manner. This fluctuation represents the capacity to adapt to changing environments, which is essential to our very survival. As managers we need to allow for and encourage diversity of thought and exploration if we are to achieve creativity and adaptability, even though operating on the edge of chaos may be quite unsettling.[14]

> The project teams that implement innovative business solutions are *complex adaptive systems* nested within companies, and large-scale complex business solutions must be easy to change as the business environment changes (i.e., adaptive). Our challenge is to learn how to employ complexity thinking to complement our conventional project management methods to manage 21st century projects.

NOTES

1. Gerry Gingrich, "Simplified Complexity: Thinking in the White Spaces," May 1998. Online at http://www.stormingmedia.us/56/5624/A562493.html (accessed January 2008).
2. Michael R. Lissack and Johan Roos, *The Next Common Sense: The e-Manager's Guide to Mastering Complexity.* (London: Nicholas Brealey Publishing, 2002).
3. D. Rind, "Complexity and Climate," *Science Magazine,* vol. 284, no. 5411 (1999), 105–107.
4. Luay Alawneh et al., "A Unified Approach for Verification and Validation of Systems and Software Engineering Models," 13th Annual IEEE International Symposium and Workshop on Engineering of Computer-Based Systems (2006), 409–418.
5. B. Michael Aucoin, *Right-Brain Project Management: A Complementary Approach* (Vienna, VA: Management Concepts, 2007), 132.

6. Roger Lewin and Birute Regine, "On the Edge in the World of Business," afterword to *Complexity: Life at the Edge of Chaos* by Roger Lewin (Chicago: University of Chicago Press, 1992), 198.

7. J. M. Ottino, "Engineering Complex Systems," *Nature* 427 (2004). Online at www.nature.com/nature (accessed January 2008).

8. Ibid.

9. M. Mitchell Waldrop, *The Emerging Science at the Edge of Order and Chaos* (New York: Simon & Schuster, 1992), 12–13.

10. Peter Fryer, "A Brief Description of Complex Adaptive Systems and Complexity Theory." Online at http://ryanlanham.wordpress.com/2007/09/01/trojanmicecom-what-are-complex-adaptive-systems (accessed January 2008).

11. Vladimir Dimitroy, "Complexity, Chaos and Creativity: A Journey Beyond System Thinking." Online at http://www.zulenet.com/VladimirDimitrov/pages/complexthink.html (accessed January 2008).

12. Peter Fryer, "A Brief Description of Complex Adaptive Systems and Complexity Theory." Online at http://www.trojanmice.com/articles/complexadaptivesystems.htm (accessed January 2008).

13. Ibid.

14. Roger Lewin and Birute Regine, *On the Edge in the World of Business,* afterword to *Complexity: Life at the Edge of Chaos* by Roger Lewin (Chicago: University of Chicago Press, 1992), 201.

CHAPTER 2
Applying Complexity Thinking to Projects

"Complexity causes confusion, which ultimately leads to failure."

—JIM CREAR, CIO, THE STANDISH GROUP INTERNATIONAL

So what do complexity, chaos, and uncertainty have to do with managing projects? As Chris Zook of Bain & Company's Global Strategy Practice contends, "As the business landscape becomes more brutal, two out of three companies will need a new business strategy to stay alive."[1]

To turn a new business strategy into reality, organizations will continually resize, restructure, reengineer, transform, and explore new models of management and leadership. Leaders around the globe are looking for ways to understand the nature of global change and to prepare for the significant transformation initiatives that will be necessary to remain competitive.

Roger Lewin and Birute Regine provide the context for complexity thinking.

ROGER LEWIN and BIRUTE REGINE
On the Edge of the Business World[2]

The business world is experiencing accelerating, revolutionary change, driven by rapid technological innovation, the globalization of business, and not least, the arrival of the Internet and the new domain of Internet commerce. The change toward what might be called "the connected economy" rivals the onset of the Industrial Revolution in its impact on society and the way commerce is transacted. Managers are finding that many of their long-established business models are inadequate to help them understand what is going on, or how to deal with it. Where managers once operated with a machine model of their world, which was predicated on linear thinking, control, and predictability, they now find themselves struggling with something more organic and nonlinear, where limited control and a restricted ability to predict are the norm.

IS CONVENTIONAL PROJECT MANAGEMENT ENOUGH?

A decade ago a major author and contributor to project management theory, Peter Morris, had this to say about the status of project management: "Project management has traditionally been thought of as the process of accomplishing a task on time, in budget, and to technical specification. Today that view is changing to something much more ambitious, exciting and challenging."[3]

Morris' first statement describes the traditional or basic project management approach—a logical, linear process to achieve a well-defined goal. The methodology for achieving that goal is well defined:

➤ Identify the problem/need (requirements)

➤ Decompose the problem into logical pieces (deliverables, work packages, activities)

➤ Do the necessary work to create these pieces (execution)

➤ Integrate the completed pieces into the final solution (validation and acceptance).

But if project management is that easy, why do major problems invariably arise in managing projects? Often, the more complex the project, the more the proponents of project management exhort project managers to follow the traditional linear approach strictly. If competence in project management disciplines is required to manage the significant change necessary to transform companies, we must ask ourselves if the current project management process is up to the challenge.

The paradigm we use to manage projects goes something like this: If we can decompose the work effort into manageable chunks of work applying *reductionism* (which postulates that complex systems can be completely understood in terms of their components[4]), we can reduce the complexity and risk, develop a plan, and then execute and rigorously control changes to the plan. Reductionist theory is the basis of many of our business management approaches, including strategic planning, business planning, performance evaluation, budgeting, and yes, project management.

Frances Storr, occupational psychologist at the Herrmann Institute, describes our changing ideas of management in her work, *That's Another Fine Mess You've Got Me Into: The Value of Chaos in Organizational Analysis.*

FRANCES STORR
That's Another Fine Mess You've Got Me Into: The Value of Chaos in Organizational Analysis[5]

The belief is that one can divide the organization's operational plan down into its component parts, allocate responsibilities, sum the resulting actions and the overall aims of the plan will be achieved. Most models of management ignore the reality of organisations as non linear feedback systems and complexity theory suggests a new approach to organisational analysis. Theories of complexity offer a new way of thinking and a new way of seeing the world. In a nonlinear system where slight variations amplify into unpredictable results, the long term future is unknowable. Therefore the skill is not to predict the future but to see patterns. . . . One should remain aware of the whole and resist analysing the parts to death.

Although complexity theory is relatively new, thought leaders and practitioners in the field of project management are beginning to embrace its tenets. The Project Management Institute (PMI®) Research Program is actively exploring the nature of complex projects and the relevance of complexity theory to project management. New project management methods and techniques that are adaptive, iterative, agile, and sometimes extreme are emerging. Leaders in the field are beginning to realize that a new paradigm is needed for managing complex projects—one that employs an adaptive method of project management versus the more conventional reductionist approach that emphasizes planning and control.

CONVENTIONAL VERSUS ADAPTIVE PROJECT MANAGEMENT

Our inclination is to manage projects using the traditional reductionist, control-based methods. Indeed, PMI's *A Guide to the Project Management Body of Knowledge (PMBOK® Guide)*,[6] which is widely accepted as the gold standard for codifying the practice of project management, presents a structured, logical approach to project management.

Using this project management model, we decompose the work into manageable components and then plan project activities in a structured manner. Once the detailed plan is created, we meticulously control changes so that we are not distracted or deterred from the plan. This works quite well for projects that are well-understood, stable, and predictable. However, 21st century projects are increasingly proving to be elusive, dynamic, and riddled with complexity. Thus, the contemporary adaptive project management model is emerging. This approach recognizes that some projects are not predictable and must be managed in a very different manner using complexity thinking, which teaches us to adapt to our environment for our very survival. In his book *Right-Brain Project Management: A Complementary Approach,* B. Michael Aucoin considers the need for an adaptive approach to project management to accommodate unpredictability on projects.

B. MICHAEL AUCOIN
Right-Brain Project Management:
A Complementary Approach[7]

A large part of what is wrong with project management is that external forces on the project demand flexibility and high performance while the dominant model for applying project management is structured. That model delivers great performance when the need is familiar and predictable, but struggles when the need is novel and ambiguous.

Twenty-first century projects are chaotic, difficult to predict, and subject to unbending time-to-market demands. Today's project teams need to deal with technology that changes constantly, global markets that are complex and evolving, ambiguous corporate strategies, and poorly understood business requirements.

Conventional project management practices, which originated in the 1950s using mathematical models and structured planning approaches, assume a stable and predictable environment.[8] Conventional project management works well and should be used for predictable, repeatable projects; however, this approach has proven to be no match for chaotic 21st century projects. Table 2-1 compares the characteristics of projects that can successfully use conventional project management practices with the characteristics of projects that require a more adaptive project management model. A blend of the two project management models is almost always the answer. The trick is to know when and how to apply which approach.

Conventional Project Management	Adaptive Project Management
Structured, orderly, disciplined	Spontaneous, disorganized
Relies heavily on plans	Evolves as more information is known
Predictable, well-defined, repeatable	Surprising, ambiguous, unique, unstable
Unwavering environment	Volatile and chaotic environment
Proven technologies	Unproven technologies
Realistic schedule	Aggressive schedule, urgent need

TABLE 2-1. Characteristics of Conventional versus Adaptive Project Management

COMPLEXITY THINKING: A RIGHT-BRAIN ACTIVITY

"Welcome a certain amount of complexity and churn because it creates a chemical reaction that jars creative thinking."

—COLLEEN YOUNG,
VP AND DISTINGUISHED ANALYST AND IT ADVISER, GARTNER

Complexity thinking is very much a right-brain activity. Aucoin tells us that the tools for mastering complex projects come from using the right brain.[9] While the left brain is dominant when applying conventional project management methods, Aucoin contends that the nature of projects today demands this new adaptive approach, which is predominantly a right-brain activity. In practice, Aucoin emphasizes that two brains are better than one: The project manager needs to develop a sense of when to apply these complementary approaches. Table 2-2 contrasts right-brain and left-brain processing styles.[10]

Left Brain	Right Brain
Verbal communication, uses words	Uses visual, spatial, tactile communication
Relies on logic	Processes emotions, offers intuition
Prefers to execute known rules	Seeks new associations, creative thought
Operates sequentially	Is comfortable with disconnected information
Prefers predictable behavior	Is comfortable with some ambiguity
Executes known patterns	Learns new unknown patterns
Prefers what is explicit, concrete	Prefers abstract concepts, metaphors
Operates with complete information	Operates with incomplete information
Unable to make decisions independently	Comfortable with critical decision-making

TABLE 2-2. Left-Brain versus Right-Brain Processing Styles

Aucoin goes on to say that left-brain techniques are perfectly appropriate for projects that are well-understood and predictable, particularly if the project team members have worked together in the past. But if the project involves new, unproven technologies or reengineered sophisticated business processes, and the team members have not worked together in the past, right-brain approaches will likely be needed as well. Aucoin concludes that it is important to truly understand the level and nature of complexity, and then to choose a more adaptive management approach for projects that involve the following:[11]

➤ Uncertainty, complexity, and urgency

➤ Expectations to achieve a reliable and predictable standard of performance, even in the midst of uncertainty and ambiguity

➤ An intricate array of people and groups.

Project managers everywhere are searching for ways to explore and understand the nature of the uncertainties and the causes of the complexity before making decisions about how to best manage a project. An understanding is emerging in the project management community that conventional project management practices are not enough when dealing with ambiguity, uncertainty, and the resulting complexities. To engage your right brain for increased agility, Aucoin gives us new insights and tools for succeeding on today's aggressive projects. Doug DeCarlo provides a succinct description of Aucoin's seven principles of right-brain project management.

DOUG DECARLO
Engaging Your Right Brain for Increased Agility[12]

In his landmark book *Right-Brain Project Management: A Complementary Approach,* author Mike Aucoin gives us new insights and tools for succeeding on today's aggressive projects. Here is a summary of Mike's Seven Principles of Right-Brain Project Management:

1. Find the compelling purpose

When a project has a compelling purpose, it unleashes motivation that otherwise would not be there. Great leaders and project managers are adept at identifying the hook that makes the project desirable. That is, they tap into the right brain. Tom Peters referred to this as the "WOW! Factor." A compelling purpose galvanizes people while giving them a sense of meaning and importance.

2. Make sense of the project

Many of today's contemporary projects are hard to figure out. Just like the ever-changing jigsaw puzzle, they are too complex for predominantly linear solutions. The role of the right brain is to discover patterns from fragmented and disjointed information. The left brain can then be enlisted to examine and test these patterns, hunches, and intuitive leaps for validity. For instance, when people are trying to get their minds around a new project or project deliverable, I often say to the group, "Think of this project as an animal, real or imagined. Draw a picture of what it would look like." Then go around and have them explain their drawings. This right-brain activity gives people a better feel for the project when the logic and linear thinking of the left get stuck.

Sense-making, as Mike Aucoin points out, applies not only to understanding the end product (deliverable), but also to the task level and process for getting there. The tools include rich communication using scenarios, metaphors, and stories.

3. Experiment and adapt

You don't manage the unknown the same way that you manage the known. When dealing with contemporary projects, by definition we often don't know enough in advance to plan with certainty. No amount of planning will eliminate uncertainty (although many have not discovered this). The left brain wants to convince us that we can plan with accuracy and thereby eliminate the need to experiment; that is, to learn by trial and error. In the right-brain world, reality rules. Not the plan. And even though we have a plan, our practice is to de-plan and re-plan constantly.

4. Create the new reality

Creativity means coming up with a new idea. Innovation means applying that idea in a productive or profitable way. Here again the right and left brain do their dance: the right side brainstorms new ideas while the left brain is asked to patiently await judgment. Later, the left side kicks into action to evaluate the idea.

5. Exercise and fulfill trust

Complex, aggressive projects cannot be led solely from the top down. There are too many moving parts for any one person to keep track of and be able to make effective decisions. Instead, leadership is best decentralized if we are to foster creativity in problem-solving and timely decision-making. All this requires trust.

6. Hit the sweet spot

The sweet spot is a place of dynamic balance between the left and right brain. "Dynamic" because the spot is constantly changing. Being in the sweet spot is a by-product of the other six principles.

7. Leave a legacy

What will be said and how will people feel after the lights have been turned off and the project has been completed? All projects leave a legacy, even if it's only in the minds of those who worked on the project. How do we want to remember this project? How do we want others to remember it? Will it be remembered with pride or with disdain? Envisioning a project's success is a powerful activity for experiencing in advance the feeling of success. This is where the right brain creates magic. Creating a powerful vision (call it leaving a legacy in advance) for your project unleashes tremendous forces that propel the project forward. For instance, imagine going into your project having already experienced (in your own mind and body) the impact that your project will have on the team, the organization, the industry, or even humanity?

This is the province and power of the right brain: It doesn't know the difference between what is imagined and what it true. It simply acts according to what is imagined and works in the background to bring the legacy into reality. The right brain provides the imagination. The left side provides the process and tools.

> **It's a Balance**
>
> You hear people say of themselves that they are right-brained or they are left-brained. What they really mean is that they are predominantly left- or right-brain oriented. Today's complex projects are predominantly right-brain ventures, but also rely on left-brain capabilities. And the balance will shift throughout the project. Agility is the ability to toggle back and forth between left- and right-brain activities. It's a dance. And you don't want to still be doing the cha cha when the music has changed to hip hop.

In the next chapter we introduce our *Project Complexity Model* and describe how best to use it as a tool to diagnose project complexity. In the remaining chapters of this book, we describe the appropriate management approaches for dealing with the various dimensions of complexity your project exhibits.

NOTES

1. Diann Daniel, "Complex IT Will Kill Your Business." Online at http://www.cio.com/article/126350/Complex_IT_Will_Kill_Your_Business (accessed May 2008).
2. Roger Lewin and Birute Regine, "On the Edge in the World of Business," afterword to *Complexity: Life at the Edge of Chaos* by Roger Lewin (Chicago: University of Chicago Press, 1992), 197.
3. Peter W. G. Morris, *Key Issues in Project Leadership: Project Management Handbook* (San Francisco: Jossey-Bass, 1998), 3.
4. WordNet (a lexical database for the English language). Cognitive Science Laboratory, Princeton University. Online at http://wordnet.princeton.edu/perl/webwn?s=reductionism (accessed January 2008).
5. Frances Storr, "That's Another Fine Mess You've Got Me Into: The Value of Chaos in Organizational Analysis." Online at http://www.trojanmice.com/index.htm. (accessed January 2008).
6. PMI and PMBOK are registered trademarks of the Project Management Institute.
7. B. Michael Aucoin, *Right-Brain Project Management: A Complementary Approach* (Vienna, VA: Management Concepts, 2007), 115–123.
8. Ibid., 122.
9. Ibid., 12.
10. Ibid., 41. © 2007 by Management Concepts, Inc. Reprinted with permission.
11. Ibid., 41.
12. Doug DeCarlo, "Engaging Your Right Brain for Increased Agility" (July 2007). Online at http://www.gantthead.com/articles/articlesPrint.cfm?ID=237412 (accessed February 2008).

CHAPTER 3

The Project Complexity Model

"Complexity, the poetry of what we know, and what we don't."

—Gerald Mulenburg, PhD
Senior Analyst, NASA Ames Research Center

"As we know,

There are knowns and unknowns.

There are known-knowns.

These are the things we know we know.

We also know there are known-unknowns.

That is to say, there are some things we know we do not know.

But there are also unknown-unknowns.

These are things that we don't know we don't know."

—Donald Rumsfeld, former U.S. Secretary of Defense

Webster's Encyclopedic Unabridged Dictionary tells us that *complexity* is characterized by a complicated or involved arrangement of many interconnected parts, units, etc., and that the situation is so complicated or intricate as to be hard to understand or deal with. In this chapter we explore the characteristics of highly complex projects and introduce our *Project Complexity Model,* which project leaders can use to diagnose the various facets and levels of complexity on a particular project.

THE NATURE OF PROJECT COMPLEXITY

The jury is still out: There is no widely accepted definition of *project complexity* that is research-based and therefore defensible.[1] The project management industry seems to be taking the stand that "You will know it when you see it." We do, however, have a good understanding of some of the sources of project complexity:[2]

> ➤ *Details*: number of variables and interfaces

> ➤ *Ambiguity:* lack of awareness of events and causality

> ➤ *Uncertainty:* inability to pre-evaluate actions

> ➤ *Unpredictability:* inability to know what will happen

> ➤ *Dynamics*: rapid rate of change

> ➤ *Social structure:* numbers and types of interactions.

We will not attempt to put forth an authoritative definition of project complexity; we leave that to the academics. However, the consensus in the industry is that a project that consists of many moving parts that are interdependent should be treated as complex. Project managers also agree that our failure to understand the complexity of the product or the project often leads us to project failure,[3] as does our inability to recognize uncertainty. Many authors stress the relationship between how well-defined goals are and how certain the methods of achieving the goals are, suggesting different managerial techniques depending on the uncertainties.[4] Others postulate that the element of urgency present on so many projects today adds its own element of complexity and stress.

IT projects are almost always complex and difficult to manage. One common source of that complexity is that IT projects often begin with limited information, when the business benefits to be achieved and what is needed to achieve them are not yet known. Another problem arises when scope is added during the development process simply because we were unable to define all requirements initially. If evaluation of what is needed and how to achieve it can be accomplished for other types of complex projects, why not for IT projects?

Models are beginning to emerge to help us understand the nature of project complexity. Two such models that are receiving a lot of attention at the National Aeronautics and Space Administration (NASA) are the UCP model (Uncertainty, Complexity, and Pace) and the NCTP model (Novelty, Complexity, Technology, and Pace), developed by Dr. Aaron J. Shenhar and colleagues. These dimensions help the project team identify where to focus its efforts[5] and give us a glimpse into the most challenged areas of modern projects.

Figure 3-1 presents the key elements of the theoretical UCP model and the practical NCTP "Diamond" model. Both of these models blend the elements of uncertainty and complexity with speed.

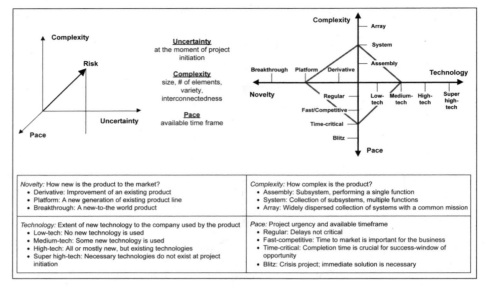

FIGURE 3-1. Theoretical UCP Model and Practical NCTP "Diamond" Model[6]

Building on existing research, we will explore what we believe is a widely accepted set of the dimensions of project complexity. The ability to identify, or "diagnose," some or all of the complexity dimensions on a project informs the project leadership team members as they make decisions about how to manage the various aspects of the project.

INTRODUCING THE PROJECT COMPLEXITY MODEL

Our *Project Complexity Model* captures the dimensions of project complexity—those characteristics that make a project unpredictable and dynamic. Depending on which dimensions apply to a particular project, the project leadership team should consider using particular project management tools, methods, and approaches.

Traditional project management tools and techniques remain quite valid, and emerging methods to manage project complexity are proving to be effective as well. The trick is to determine which approaches and interventions to apply when. Our approach seeks to add value to the project by affording the project team the ability to adapt to developing information and changes in the environment and to fine tune the project methods accordingly.

The *Project Complexity Model* presented in Table 3-1 offers a framework for identifying and diagnosing the elements of complexity on a particular project so that the project team can make appropriate management decisions. The model captures a number of dimensions of project complexity, including project time and value; team size and composition; urgency; schedule, cost, and scope flexibility; clarity of the problem and solution; stability of requirements; strategic importance; stakeholder influence; level of organizational and commercial change; external constraints and dependencies; political sensitivity; and unproven technology.

USING THE PROJECT COMPLEXITY MODEL

Before examining the model, it is important to understand that relatively small, short-duration projects might be highly complex because they exhibit dimensions of complexity that have nothing to do with size, e.g., the level of change required within both the business and technical communities. In the case of large-scale organizational change, deployment across multicultural groups can make the project complex even if the new business solution is relatively straightforward. The model is meant to be applied in its entirety, considering the confluence and interaction of numerous dimensions.

To use the model to diagnose the complexity of a particular project, shade the boxes that best describe your project and apply the complexity formula presented in Table 3-2. Note that not all conditions described in a box need to be present; shade only the one cell in each row that best describes your project. While the model can be used on all project types, we designed it to best fit typical projects in the business environment.

Complexity Dimensions	Project Complexity Profile		
	Independent	**Moderately Complex**	**Highly Complex**
Time/Cost	< 3 months < $250K	3–6 months $250K–$750K	> 6 months > $750K
Team Size	3–4 team members	5–10 team members	> 10 team members
Team Composition and Performance	• Strong project leadership • Team staffed internally, has worked together in the past, and has a track record of reliable estimates • Formal, proven PM, BA, and SE methodology with QA and QC processes defined and operational	• Competent project leadership • Team staffed with internal and external resources; internal staff has worked together in the past and has track record of reliable estimates • Contract for external resources is straightforward; contractor performance is known • Semi-formal methodology with QA/QC processes defined	• Project manager inexperienced in leading complex projects • Complex team structure of varying competencies (e.g., contractor, virtual, culturally diverse, outsourced) • Complex contracts; contractor performance unknown • Diverse methodologies
Urgency and Flexibility of Cost, Time, and Scope	• Minimized scope • Small milestones • Flexible schedule, budget, and scope	• Schedule, budget, and scope can undergo minor variations, but deadlines are firm • Achievable scope and milestones	• Over-ambitious schedule and scope • Deadline is aggressive, fixed, and cannot be changed • Budget, scope, and quality have no room for flexibility
Clarity of Problem, Opportunity, and Solution	• Clear business objectives • Easily understood problem, opportunity, or solution	• Defined business objectives • Problem or opportunity is partially defined • Solution is partially defined	• Unclear business objectives • Problem or opportunity is ambiguous and undefined • Solution is difficult to define
Requirements Volatility and Risk	• Strong customer/user support • Basic requirements are understood, straightforward, and stable	• Adequate customer/user support • Basic requirements are understood but are expected to change • Moderately complex functionality	• Inadequate customer/user support • Requirements are poorly understood, volatile, and largely undefined • Highly complex functionality

Complexity Dimensions	Project Complexity Profile		
	Independent	**Moderately Complex**	**Highly Complex**
Strategic Importance, Political Implications, Multiple Stakeholders	• Strong executive support • No political implications • Straightforward communications	• Adequate executive support • Some direct impact on mission • Minor political implications • 2–3 stakeholder groups • Challenging communication and coordination effort	• Mixed/inadequate executive support • Impact on core mission • Major political implications • Visible at highest levels of the organization • Multiple stakeholder groups with conflicting expectations
Level of Organizational Change	• Impacts a single business unit, one familiar business process, and one IT system	• Impacts 2–3 somewhat familiar business units, processes, and IT systems	• Large-scale organizational change that impacts the enterprise • Spans functional groups or agencies • Shifts or transforms the organization • Impacts many business processes and IT systems
Level of Commercial Change	• Minor changes to existing commercial practices	• Enhancements to existing commercial practices	• Groundbreaking commercial practices
Risks, Dependencies, and External Constraints	• Considered low risk • Some external influences • No challenging integration issues • No new or unfamiliar regulatory requirements • No punitive exposure	• Considered moderate risk • Some project objectives are dependent on external factors • Challenging integration effort • Some new regulatory requirements • Acceptable exposure	• Considered high risk • Overall project success depends largely on external factors • Significant integration required • Highly regulated or novel sector • Significant exposure
Level of IT Complexity	• Solution is readily achievable using existing, well-understood technologies • IT complexity is low	• Solution is difficult to achieve or technology is proven but new to the organization • IT complexity and legacy integration are moderate	• Solution requires groundbreaking innovation • Solution is likely to use immature, unproven, or complex technologies provided by outside vendors • IT complexity and legacy integration are high

TABLE 3-1. Project Complexity Model

Highly Complex	Moderately Complex	Independent
Level of change = large-scale enterprise impacts *or* Both the problem and the solution are difficult to define or understand, and the solution is difficult to achieve. The solution is likely to use unproven technologies. *or* Four or more categories in the "highly complex" column	Two or more categories in the "moderately complex" column *or* One category in the "highly complex" column and three or more in the "moderately complex" column	No more than one category in the "moderately complex" column *and* No categories in the "highly complex" column

TABLE 3-2. Project Complexity Formula

RATIONALE FOR THE PROJECT COMPLEXITY MODEL

The *Project Complexity Model* is robust, encompassing the priorities emphasized in the Standish Group's *Recipe for Project Success: The CHAOS Ten* as well as the best practices presented in the nine knowledge areas of the *PMBOK® Guide*: scope, time, cost, integration, procurement, quality, communication, risk, and human resource management.[7]

Several variations of project assessment models are available in the project management literature. In their *Project Sizing Grid,* for example, David Hillson and Peter Simon[8] present four levels of project characteristics to arrive at an overall project risk rating. Depending on whether the project is considered small, medium, or large, the appropriate level of risk management activities can be determined.

Another model is Gregory Garrett's *Project Complexity Assessment Tool.*[9] Garrett uses five levels of project complexity characteristics (low, low-to-medium, medium, medium-to-high, and high) to extrapolate the level of project complexity and thereby determine the level of project management rigor that is needed to achieve success.

We have chosen to use a clear-cut three-tiered model for simplicity and ease of use. Referencing the model, some may argue that a project needs to be much longer in duration than six months or much larger in value than $750K to be considered complex. However, we have chosen these tolerances based on project performance statistics that clearly indicate that projects of this size involving new or changed IT systems are complex and challenging. Standish CHAOS research shows that we have been able to improve performance by reducing project duration and resource levels. Our approach is consistent with the *Recipe for Project Success* put forth by The Standish Group International in 1999 and updated in 2001 (depicted in Table 3-3).[10] The message is clear: Size matters; less is more.

Ingredients	Clear business objective; minimized scope (microprojects with rigorous configuration management); communication and collaboration; proven, standard, stable software infrastructure (versus custom code); firm basic requirements; formal methodology; reliable estimates
Mix with	Full-time, co-located core team members (experienced business analyst, project manager, business visionary, architects, and developers) coached by an involved executive project sponsor
Bake	No longer than six months; no more than six people; no more than $750,000 (1999) No longer than four months; no more than four people; no more than $500,000 (2001)

TABLE 3-3. Standish Group Recipe for Project Success

VISUALIZING PROJECT COMPLEXITY

To communicate the nature of the complexities on your project, it is helpful to create a visual to accompany the tabular version of the model depicting overall project complexity by developing a "spider chart." The example in Figure 3-2 depicts a project that is highly complex based the team composition, urgent need, requirements volatility, political sensitivity, and level of organizational change.

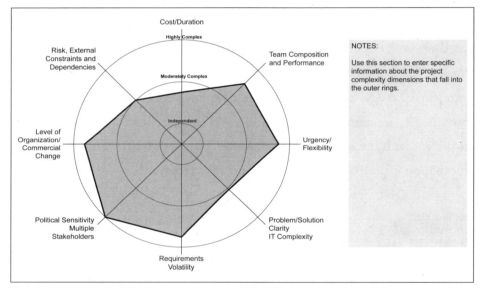

FIGURE 3-2. Spider Chart Depicting Overall Project Complexity

Figure 3-3 presents a view of the *Project Complexity Model* that incorporates the concept of program management. A program is a group of related projects that exhibit varying degrees of complexity. As you diagnose the complexity of each project within the program, it is wise to focus on the high-risk, highly complex projects first to ensure that their risks and complexities can be managed before time and resources are invested on the less complex projects.

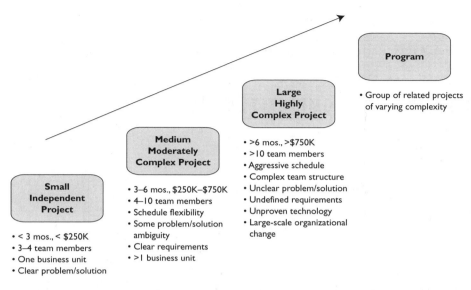

FIGURE 3-3. Project and Program Complexity Model

WHEN TO APPLY COMPLEXITY THINKING TO PROJECTS

The *Project Complexity Model* can be used to guide the management of complex projects during many phases of the project life cycle. Take your project leadership team through the analysis recommended in the remaining sections of this book to apply complexity thinking to the major decisions you make about your project. Specifically, determine which project complexity management approaches to adopt when you are:

➤ Preparing the business case for a new project proposal

➤ Initiating and planning a new project

➤ Initiating and planning a new major phase of a project

➤ Recovering a troubled project

➤ Initiating and planning a new program

➤ Recovering troubled projects within a program.

HOW TO APPLY COMPLEXITY THINKING TO PROJECTS

"Fools ignore complexity,
Pragmatists suffer it,
Some can avoid it,
Geniuses remove it."

—ALAN PERLIS, AMERICAN COMPUTER SCIENTIST

For 21st century projects, it is important that the leadership team clearly understand the level of complexity and then apply a management approach that is commensurate with the project's complexity dimensions. Applying complexity thinking to projects involves selecting appropriate methods and techniques, assigning project leadership based on the project profile and complexity dimensions, and building complex, adaptive business solutions that are amenable to change as business needs evolve. The three steps in this process are listed below and are discussed in detail in the remaining parts of this book.

STEP 1: ASSIGN PROJECT LEADERS BASED ON THE PROJECT PROFILE

Projects sometimes fail because of an inappropriate match of project leadership to the level of project complexity. The project manager, business analyst, lead IT architect and developer, and business visionary are four critical project leadership positions. Once the project's complexity level and dimensions are understood, organizations should use this vital information to make project leadership assignments, as described in Part II.

STEP 2: SELECT THE PROJECT CYCLE BASED ON THE PROJECT PROFILE

Based on the project profile diagnosed using the *Project Complexity Model*, the project team determines the appropriate project cycle to use, as described in Part III. All projects have a cycle, or a sequence of stages through which the project passes. Typical cycles have a series of periods and phases, each with a defined output that guides research, development, construction, and acquisition of goods and services.[11] As projects have become more complex, project cycles have evolved to address the various levels of complexity.

STEP 3: SELECT APPROPRIATE MANAGEMENT TECHNIQUES BASED ON COMPLEXITY DIMENSIONS

Projects sometimes fail because of the misapplication of good management methods and techniques. In Part IV, we discuss the application of complexity thinking to determine the appropriate techniques to use based on the complexity dimensions present. Successful managers of complex projects become situational project managers by adapting their leadership style and the project management, software engineering, and business analysis methods they use to deal with the project's complexity dimensions.

Most 21st century business projects are highly complex, involving lots of interrelationships, nested systems within systems, and changing requirements. Using a comprehensive *Project Complexity Model* to diagnose the complexity of a particular project and making managerial decisions accordingly will greatly increase your chances of project success. We propose using the *Project Complexity Model* as a framework to inform your decisions and communicate about your project when you are:

- Assigning key project team members
- Selecting the project cycle
- Selecting appropriate management techniques based on complexity dimensions.

NOTES

1. S. Jonathan Whitty and Harvey Maylor, "And Then Came Complex Project Management," presented at the 21st IPMA World Congress on Project Management (February 2007). Online at http://espace.library.uq.edu.au/eserv.php?pid=UQ:13419&dsID=And_then_came_Complex_Project_Management.pdf (accessed January 2008).
2. Jerry Mulenburg, "What Does Complexity Have to Do With It? Complexity and the Management of Projects," From the proceedings of the 2008 NASA Project Management Challenge Conference (2008).
3. Terry Williams, *Modelling Complex Projects* (West Sussex, UK: John Wiley & Sons, Ltd., 2002), 49.
4. Ibid., 55.
5. Aaron Shenhar and Dov Dvir, *Reinventing Project Management: The Diamond Approach to Successful Growth and Innovation* (Boston: Harvard Business School Press, 2007), 15, 222.
6. Aaron J. Shenhar, "Building a Strategic System Approach to NASA's Project and Program Management," *Phase I Final Report: Identifying NASA-Specific Strategic Project Types* (December 2004).
7. Project Management Institute, *A Guide to the Project Management Body of Knowledge, Third Edition* (Newtown Square, PA: Project Management Institute, 2004).
8. David Hillson and Peter Simon, *Practical Project Risk Management: The ATOM Methodology* (Vienna, VA: Management Concepts, 2007), 29.
9. Gregory A. Garrett, *Managing Complex Outsourced Projects* (Chicago: CCH Incorporated, 2004), 72.
10. The Standish Group International, Inc., "CHAOS: A Recipe for Success," *Extreme CHAOS* (1999).
11. Hal Mooz, Kevin Forsberg and Howard Cotterman, *Communicating Project Management* (Hoboken, NJ: John Wiley & Sons, 2003), 259.

CONCLUSION TO PART I

Although our ability to manage complex, large-scale projects is improving, we clearly must find new ways to dramatically improve project performance if we are to remain competitive in the global marketplace. To enable us to adapt to the change that is all around us, project management experts and leaders are exploring the concepts of complexity theory as a complement to conventional project management approaches.

AARON J. SHENHAR and DOV DVIR
Reinventing Project Management[1]

The critical questions are these: Can we help project teams make the right assessment before presenting their project proposals to management? Can we show executives how to ask the right questions and foresee danger before they make a commitment to a project and before it is too late? And can we guide project teams in adapting their project management style to circumstances, environment, and task? It seems that managers at all levels need a new framework and a new language to communicate with each other about projects.

NOTE

1. Aaron Shenhar and Dov Dvir, *Reinventing Project Management: The Diamond Approach to Successful Growth and Innovation* (Boston: Harvard Business School Press, 2007), 8.

PART II

Applying Complexity Thinking to Assign Key Project Team Members

P rojects sometimes fail because the key project leadership positions are filled with individuals who are not sufficiently skilled and practiced to make the appropriate managerial decisions about the project, build and sustain a high-performing project team, and adapt to changes as the project unfolds. The *Project Complexity Model* can be used to make appropriate leadership assignments on a complex project.

In Chapter 4 we present the competencies required to manage complex projects—both traditional and emerging skills. In addition, we discuss the various members of the project leadership team and the need for collaborative team leadership.

In Chapter 5 we present a typical career path for project leaders and a career path for emerging managers of complex projects. A proven model for successful leaders of organizations is reviewed and applied to leaders of projects. Finally, we describe the process of assigning project leaders to complex projects using our model.

CHAPTER 4

Competencies Required to Manage Complex Projects

The Australian Defence Materiel Organisation expresses a contemporary viewpoint regarding complex projects: "It is broadly accepted that complex projects require a very different set of competencies. . . . Complex projects are characterized by uncertainty, non-linearity, and recursiveness, and are best viewed as dynamic and evolving systems."[1]

What makes a project manager competent? In this chapter we consider the different competencies needed for the senior project manger and explore the emerging understanding of the competencies needed for the complex project manager.

INDUSTRY REQUIREMENTS FOR SENIOR PROJECT LEADERS

Considerable knowledge, skill, and experience are required to manage projects. Table 4-1 presents the array of competencies involved in leading projects, including technical, analytical, business, and leadership expertise.

Technical	Analytical	Business	Leadership
Demonstrated mastery of project and program management knowledge and skills	Demonstrated mastery of business analysis knowledge and skills	Demonstrated mastery of business transformation and cultural change concepts and skills	Demonstrated mastery of portfolio management
Keen understanding of the use of technology to support business objectives	Use of project life cycles to deliver valuable solutions quickly	Strategic planning, goal setting, corporate goal measurement	Customer relationship management
Mastery of systems engineering concepts and principles	Demonstrated mastery of research studies (benchmark study, competitive analysis, feasibility analysis, market research)	Demonstrated mastery of six sigma, business process improvement and reengineering	Demonstrated mastery of management of power and politics
Powerful modeling techniques	Ability to conceptualize and think creatively	Business planning	Capacity to formulate and articulate vision
Communication of technical concepts to non-technical audiences	Techniques to plan, elicit, analyze, specify, validate, trace, and manage requirements	Communication of business concepts to technical audiences	Organizational change management
Testing, verification, and validation	Risk assessment and management	Business outcome thinking	Problem-solving, negotiation, decision-making
Technical writing	Administrative, analytical, and reporting skills	Business writing	Team management, leadership, mentoring, facilitation, meeting management
Rapid prototyping	Cost/benefit analysis	Business case development	Authenticity, ethics, integrity
Technical domain knowledge	Time and cost management, personal effectiveness	Business domain knowledge	Project benefits management

TABLE 4-1. Skill Requirements for Senior Project Leaders

In addition, we can look to the *Project Manager Competency Development Framework*[2] published by PMI for an exhaustive assessment of project management competencies. This PMI® standard discusses several dimensions of competency that are needed for successful project performance, including project management knowledge competence, project management personal competence, and project management performance competence:

➤ *Project management knowledge competence*—the knowledge and understanding that a project manager brings to a project. This competence is broken down into units, organized according to the PMI *PMBOK® Guide* knowledge areas, and further divided into clusters organized around the *PMBOK® Guide* five core process areas.

➤ *Project management personal competence*—organized into six distinct areas of competence:

  ❯ Achievement and action

  ❯ Helping and human services

  ❯ Impact and influence

  ❯ Managerial

  ❯ Cognitive

  ❯ Personal effectiveness.

➤ *Project management performance competence*—the ability to perform project management activities to the levels of performance expected.

EMERGING COMPLEX PROJECT LEADER REQUIREMENTS

Complex projects demand an exceptional level of leadership. As key project leaders are assigned to complex projects, we need to make sure they are equipped with the knowledge and skills they need to meet the challenge.

THE COMPLEX PROJECT MANAGER

As a project-oriented organization since its creation by President Eisenhower in 1958, NASA offers many insights into the fundamental characteristics of complex project managers. NASA project managers exhibit attributes similar to those found in CEOs and leaders in general. Two studies, separated by more than two decades, identified key differences between average and superior project managers.[3] Both listed personal skills in managing others as highly important for superior project managers. Two additional studies that looked at the personality characteristics of NASA project managers found a strong tendency on the Myers-Briggs Type Indicator (MBTI®) for extraversion, thinking, and judgment, with a prevalence of intuition/sensing in superior or effective project managers.[4]

STANDARDS FOR THE COMPLEX PROJECT MANAGER

Looking to another source, the Commonwealth of Australia Department of Defense issued Version 2 of the *Competency Standard for Complex Project Managers* in September 2006, which proclaims itself a ". . . milestone in the development of complex project management as a profession." The standard identifies new project management competencies with the hope of recognizing potential complex project managers early in their careers and establishing courses and development tracks to ensure that a sufficient number of complex project managers are available to meet the demand.[5] The standard has generated significant public interest in the project management community and is now out for public comment.[6]

The competencies for the complex project manager are defined in terms of role descriptions, actions in the workplace, and the underlying knowledge needed. These nine new competency areas are far-reaching:

➤ Strategy and project management

➤ Business planning, lifecycle management, reporting, and performance measurement

➤ Change and journey

➤ Innovation, creativity, and working smarter

➤ Organizational architecture

➤ Systems thinking and integration

➤ Leadership

➤ Culture and being human

➤ Probity and governance.

THE IDEAL PROJECT MANAGER

Finally, we look to J. Davidson Frame, who has conducted informal surveys of hundreds of project managers to shed light on the traits of great project managers. According to Frame, great project managers:[7]

➤ Have a thorough understanding of project goals

➤ Are capable of understanding staff needs

➤ Have a good head for details

➤ Have a strong commitment to the project

➤ Are able to cope with setbacks and disappointments

➤ Possess good negotiation skills

➤ Are results-oriented and practical

➤ Are cost-conscious and possess basic business skills

➤ Are politically savvy, aware of what not to do as well as what to do

➤ Have a high tolerance for ambiguity.

ORGANIZE FOR SUCCESS: THE CORE COMPLEX PROJECT LEADERSHIP TEAM

In an attempt to deliver projects successfully, we have traditionally focused on *management* and virtually excluded the vital role of *leadership*. As we have seen, traditionally the project manager focuses on planning, budgeting, organizing, staffing, monitoring, and controlling. All project team members report to the project manager regarding project work assigned to them. (Figure 4-1 depicts a traditional project team configuration.) It is now becoming clear that complex projects thrive on collaboration, teams, and leadership rather than command and control. In the 21st century, managing projects is transitioning from project management to team leadership.

Consider the core project leadership team concept represented in Figure 4-2. Using this concept, the leadership team is small (four to six members), multidisciplined, highly skilled, dedicated to the project full time, and co-located. The core team of experts forms sub-teams and brings in subject matter experts when needed. The members of this core leadership team share responsibility for guiding the project, each taking the lead when his or her expertise is needed.

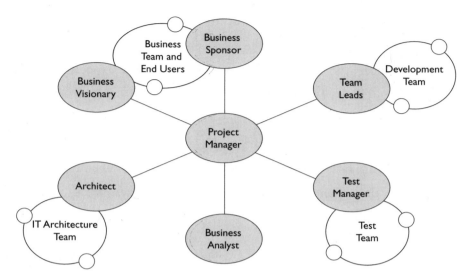

FIGURE 4-1. Traditional Project Team Configuration

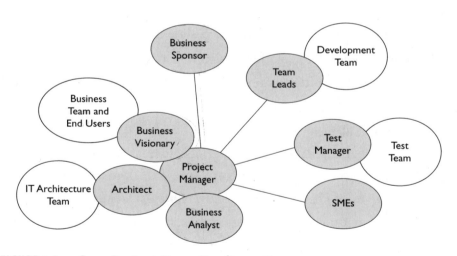

FIGURE 4-2. Core Project Team Configuration

Make no mistake, shared leadership (sometimes referred to as distributed leadership) does not mean no accountability. The project manager is still responsible for ensuring that the business solution is delivered on time, on budget, and with the full scope promised. The business analyst is responsible for ensuring that the project team fully understands the business need and the benefits expected from the new solution, and for validating that the solution meets the requirements and will deliver the expected business benefits. The architect ensures that the solution is optimal and is designed and developed according to specifications. The business visionary keeps the team focused on the big picture (the strategic goal that will be advanced by the new solution), brings in appropriate business experts when needed, and helps prepare the organization to operate in a new way once the business solution is deployed.

Whereas in the past project teams revolved around the project manager as their leader, the very nature of project team leadership is changing. Leadership within the team shifts subtly based on where the project is in its life cycle. For example, during requirements elicitation, the business analyst takes the lead and the other core team members slide into more of a support role. As the project moves into solution design and development, the technical architect or developer often assumes the lead role. All core leadership team members support each other—and get out of the way when their expertise is not the critical element.

Complex projects demand an exceptional level of management and, perhaps even more important, leadership. An array of project management competencies is required to manage complex projects, some of which we have traditionally expected of our senior project managers. The additional competencies required for project leaders to be able to lead complex projects successfully are just now emerging. Clearly, a collaborative team of experts is needed to lead complex 21st century projects.

NOTES

1. DCEO, "Project Management Competencies for Complex Projects," DCEO Speech to Pro-MAC2006. Online at http://www.defence.gov.au/dmo/speeches_other/dceo_promac_2006.pdf (accessed March 2008).

2. Project Management Institute, *A Guide to the Project Management Body of Knowledge,* Third Edition (Newtown Square, PA: Project Management Institute, 2004).

3. R. L. Chapman, "Project Management in NASA: The System and the Men," National Aeronautics and Space Administration, NASA SP-324 (1973); D. Leonard, M. Fambrough, and R. Boyatzis, "Project Management at NASA's Lewis Research Center: Identifying a Model of Superior Performance," National Aeronautics and Space Administration, NASA Grant: NCC-3-90, LSN: 10414 (1995).

4. C. R. Dreyfus, "Scientists and Engineers as Effective Managers: A Study of the Development of Interpersonal Abilities," Unpublished doctoral dissertation, Case Western Reserve University (1991); G. M. Mulenburg, "The Characteristics of Project Managers: An Exploration of Complex Projects in the National Aeronautics and Space Administration," NASA/TP-2000-209593.

5. Commonwealth of Australia (Department of Defence), College of Complex Project Managers and Defence Materiel Organisation, "Competency Standard for Complex Project Managers," Public Release Version 2.0 (2006). Online at http://www.defence.gov.au/dmo/proj_man/Complex_PM_v2.0.pdf (accessed January 2008).

6. S. Jonathan Whitty and Harvey Maylor, "And Then Came Complex Project Management," presented at the 21st IPMA World Congress on Project Management (February 2007). Online at http://espace.library.uq.edu.au/eserv.php?pid=UQ:13419&dsID=And_then_came_Complex_Project_Management.pdf (accessed January 2008).

7. J. Davidson Frame, *The New Project Management: Tools for an Age of Rapid Change, Complexity, and Other Business Realities* (San Francisco: Jossey-Bass, 2002), 12–13.

CHAPTER 5

Developing Leaders of Complex Projects

As organizations depend more and more on project outcomes to achieve their strategic goals, they are developing career paths for their project leadership positions, including project managers, business analysts, lead technologists (architects and developers), and business visionaries. Organizations that are undergoing pivotal transitions require leaders who exhibit characteristics and follow a career path that differs in certain respects from the characteristics and career path of traditional project leaders. Complexity thinking can assist organizations in identifying and developing these leaders.

TRADITIONAL PROJECT LEADER CAREER PATH

The traditional project leader career path starts with entry-level associates who are mainly in support positions and transitions to strategic-level project leaders who lead critical, complex projects (Table 5-1).

Level	Proficiency	Responsibilities	Competencies
Strategic	• Ability to perform strategic tasks with minimal direction	• Lead large, highly complex projects	• Business and IT strategy • Program and portfolio management • Systems engineering, BPR, six sigma • Enterprise architecture • Business case development
Senior	• Ability to perform complex tasks with minimal coaching	• Lead moderately complex projects	• Business and IT domains • Advanced project management and business analysis • Systems engineering, BPR, six sigma • Requirements engineering
Intermediate	• Ability to perform simple to moderately complex tasks with minimal assistance	• Lead small, independent projects	• Business or IT domain • Fundamentals of project management and business analysis • Quality management • Facilitation and meeting management • Basic requirements modeling
Associate	• Ability to perform simple tasks with assistance	• Support intermediate and senior PMs/ BAs	• PM/BA principles • BPR, six sigma principles • Business writing

TABLE 5-1. Traditional Project Leader Career Path

EMERGING COMPLEX PROJECT MANAGER CAREER PROGRESSION

The Australian *Competency Standard for Complex Project Managers* proposes a new four-tiered career path:

➤ Project manager

➤ Traditional senior project manager

➤ Program manager

➤ Complex project manager.

While this structure is not yet fully accepted in the project management community, it is certainly food for thought as we consider the competencies needed to manage complex projects successfully. The standard also proposes certification levels for traditional and complex project managers (Table 5-2) and describes four competency levels for each action in the workplace (Table 5-3).[1]

Traditional			Complex	
Project Manager	Senior Project Manager	Program Manager	Member	Fellow

TABLE 5-2. Complex Project Manager Certification Levels

Traditional				Complex	
Actions in Workplace	Project Manager	Senior Project Manager	Program Manager	Member	Fellow
Develops vision statement, values charter, code of conduct, and mission statement	D	D	P	C	L
Maps stakeholder alignment/ differences over the project life cycle	D	D	P	C	L

Key:
D – development
P – practitioner
C – competent
L – leader

TABLE 5-3. Complex Project Manager Competency Model

For each action in the workplace, certification levels are defined as follows:

➤ *Development.* The project manager applies the competency under direct supervision.

➤ *Practitioner.* The project manager applies the competency without the need for direct supervision, but within the bounds of standardized processes, procedures, and systems.

➤ *Competent.* The project manager applies the competency without the need for direct supervision, provides direct supervision of the competency for others, and mentors development of the competency in others.

➤ *Leader.* The project manager provides professional leadership in the competency; leads in the design of processes, procedures, and systems; and has the ability to use the competency flexibly and creatively.

SUCCESSFUL LEADERSHIP CHARACTERISTICS FOR ORGANIZATIONS UNDERGOING PIVOTAL TRANSITIONS

As we work to identify and develop leaders of complex projects, we examine a model for exceptional organizational leadership presented by Jim Collins. Collins provides us with researched-based information on the characteristics of business leaders whose companies are exceptionally successful during pivotal transition periods; these characteristics are also relevant to project leaders who are successful in leading complex projects.

Collins describes these leaders as very ambitious but also very humble. Their ambition is first for the organization rather than for themselves, and their goal is to leave the legacy of a successful enterprise. Characteristics of these leaders, which Collins refers to as "level 5 leaders," include a compelling personal humility coupled with an unwavering resolve that he calls "professional will." Collins describes a leader with personal humility as someone who:[2]

➤ Demonstrates a compelling modesty, virtually shunning public praise

➤ Acts with quiet, calm determination

➤ Channels ambitions into the company; identifies and mentors successors for even greater success

➤ Attributes success to others.

A leader who exhibits professional will:

➤ Creates superb results

➤ Demonstrates an unwavering resolve to do whatever it takes to produce the best long-term results for the enterprise

➤ Sets the standard of building an enduring great company

➤ Attributes responsibility for poor results to himself.

We submit that leaders of complex projects should strive to become level 5 leaders, doing whatever it takes to produce the best long-term results. We have adapted Collins' path to level 5 leadership to depict the path to becoming a complex project leader (see Table 5-4).

Leadership Level	Leadership Characteristics
Level 1	**Highly Capable Individual** Contributes to project success through individual expertise, talent, knowledge, skills, and good work habits
Level 2	**Contributing Team Member** Contributes individual capabilities to the achievement of business objectives and works effectively with others
Level 3	**Competent Project Leader** Organizes people and resources toward the effective and efficient pursuit of business objectives
Level 4	**Exceptional Project Leader** Commits to vigorous pursuit of a clear and compelling project vision, stimulating higher performance standards with a track record of project success

Level 5	**Complex Project Leader** Brings about business transformation in pursuit of new business strategies through personal and professional leadership

TABLE 5-4. Complex Project Leader Development Path

USING COMPLEXITY THINKING TO ASSIGN COMPLEX PROJECT LEADERS

To make the most appropriate project leadership assignments, management must consider project complexity. Figure 5-1 maps the generic career levels presented earlier with the project profiles contained in our *Project Complexity Model.* As depicted, strategic-level leaders are needed to manage not only highly complex projects, but programs (groups of projects managed in a coordinated way to obtain greater benefits) and portfolios (collections of projects or programs managed together to achieve strategic goals) as well.

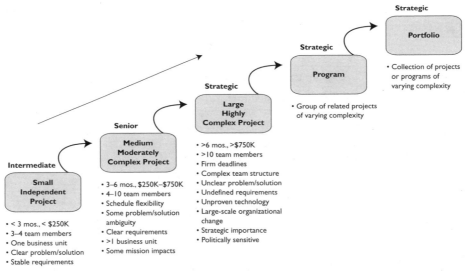

FIGURE 5-1. Project Leadership Capability Maturity Model

Organizations are recognizing that complex projects require an exceptional leadership *team of experts* and are developing career paths for their project leadership positions—project managers, business analysts, lead technologists (architects and developers), and business visionaries—accordingly.

Based on the project profile diagnosed using the *Project Complexity Model,* organizations undergoing pivotal transitions can apply complexity thinking when considering assignments for complex project leaders. Projects need no longer fail because the key project leadership positions are filled with individuals who are not sufficiently skilled and practiced to make the appropriate managerial decisions about the project, build and sustain a high-performing project team, and adapt to changes as the project unfolds.

NOTES

1. Commonwealth of Australia (Department of Defence), College of Complex Project Managers and Defence Materiel Organisation, "Competency Standard for Complex Project Managers," Public Release Version 2.0 (2006). Online at http://www.defence.gov.au/dmo/proj_man/Complex_PM_v2.0.pdf (accessed January 2008), 17–18.
2. Jim Collins, *Good to Great: Why Some Companies Make the Leap...and Others Don't* (New York: HarperCollins Publishers, Inc., 2001), 36.

CONCLUSION TO PART II

Projects no longer need fail because key leadership positions are filled with individuals who are not up to the challenge. In Part II we presented the information organizations need to make effective leadership assignments for complex projects. We proposed that:

➤ Complex projects require collaborative team leadership, not simply a senior project manager

➤ Career paths to develop leaders of complex projects are emerging

➤ Proven models exist for successful leaders of organizations that can be readily applied to leaders of complex projects

➤ Using the *Project Complexity Model* to assign project managers and other key project leadership positions will help ensure that you get "the right stuff" on your team.

PART III

Applying Complexity Thinking to Select the Project Cycle

Based on the project profile diagnosed using the *Project Complexity Model,* and after the core project leadership team is established, the team collaborates to determine the appropriate project cycle to use. All projects have a cycle, a sequence of stages through which the project passes. Typical cycles comprise a series of periods and phases, each with a defined output that guides research, development, construction, and acquisition of goods and services.[1]

Project cycle models (also referred to as project life cycle models) are not interchangeable, and one size does not fit all. As projects have become more complex, project cycles have evolved to address the various levels of complexity. It is important to know the complexity of your project and to apply the approach that is best suited to manage or reduce that complexity.

Project cycles can be categorized into broad types:[2]

➤ *Linear:* used when the business problem, opportunity, and solution are clear, no major changes are expected, and the effort is considered to be routine. A linear cycle is typically used for maintenance, enhancement, and continuous process improvement projects. It is also used for development projects when requirements are well-understood and stable, as in shrink-wrap software development projects.

➤ *Incremental:* used when the effort is well-understood and only moderately complex, but the customer wants to deploy value incrementally. An incremental cycle can also be used for maintenance, enhancement, and continuous process improvement projects.

➤ *Iterative:* used when the requirements are unclear, incomplete, or subject to change. An iterative cycle is typically used for technology development projects.

➤ *Adaptive:* used when the business problem, opportunity, and solution are unclear and the schedule is aggressive. An adaptive cycle is typically used for new technology development, new product development, or complex business process reengineering projects.

➤ *Extreme:* used when the business objectives are unclear and the solution is undefined. An extreme cycle is typically used for research and development, new technology, and new product development projects.

As we move along the continuum from independent to highly complex projects, the appropriate project cycles move from linear to iterative to adaptive and even to extreme approaches to manage the uncertainties (Figure III-1).

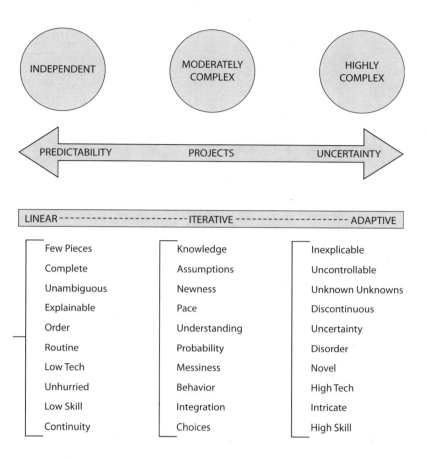

FIGURE III-1. Project Complexity Mapped to Project Cycle Approaches

In this part we examine the appropriate project cycles to use based on the project profile diagnosed using the *Project Complexity Model:*

➤ In Chapter 6 we examine the appropriate project cycles for independent projects.

➤ In Chapter 7 we examine the appropriate project cycles for moderately complex projects.

➤ In Chapter 8 we examine the appropriate project cycles for highly complex projects.

NOTES

1. Hal Mooz, Kevin Forsberg, and Howard Cotterman, *Communicating Project Management* (Hoboken, NJ: John Wiley & Sons, 2003), 259.
2. Robert K. Wysocki, *Effective Project Management: Traditional, Adaptive, Extreme, Fourth Edition* (Indianapolis, IN: Wiley Publishing, Inc., 2007), 48.

CHAPTER 6
Appropriate Project Cycles for Independent Projects

As depicted in the *Project Complexity Model,* independent business projects are typically of short duration and are staffed with competent project leadership and internal team members (two to four team members) who have worked together in the past, use repeatable processes, and have a track record of reliable estimates. Scope has been minimized, and both the schedule and budget have some flexibility.

The business objective on an independent project is clear, requirements are well-defined and stable, and the solution is readily achievable using existing, well-understood technology. In addition, the project has strong executive support, few stakeholders, and no political implications. Minimal organizational change is involved, affecting only one business unit, one familiar business process, or one IT system undergoing maintenance or enhancement. No new or unfamiliar regulatory requirements or punitive exposures are being addressed, and the IT complexity is low. Table 6-1 presents the complexity profile of an independent project.

Complexity Dimensions	Complexity Profile of an Independent Project
Time/Cost	< 3 months < $250K
Team Size	3–4 team members
Team Composition and Performance	• Strong project leadership • Team staffed internally, has worked together in the past, and has a track record of reliable estimates • Formal, proven PM, BA, and SE methodology with QA and QC processes defined and operational
Urgency and Flexibility of Cost, Time, and Scope	• Minimized scope • Small milestones • Flexible schedule, budget, and scope
Clarity of Problem, Opportunity, and Solution	• Clear business objectives • Easily understood problem, opportunity, or solution
Requirements Volatility and Risk	• Strong customer/user support • Basic requirements are understood, straightforward, and stable
Strategic Importance, Political Implications, Multiple Stakeholders	• Strong executive support • No political implications • Straightforward communications
Level of Organizational Change	• Impacts a single business unit, one familiar business process, and one IT system
Level of Commercial Change	• Minor changes to existing commercial practices
Risks, Dependencies, and External Constraints	• Considered low risk • Some external influences • No challenging integration issues • No new or unfamiliar regulatory requirements • No punitive exposure
Level of IT Complexity	• Solution is readily achievable using existing, well-understood technologies • IT complexity is low

TABLE 6-1. Complexity Profile of an Independent Project

In Figure 6-1, we see that with the exception of one complexity dimension, urgency/flexibility, our *Project Complexity Formula* (reproduced here as Table 6-2) tells us that this should be managed as an independent project.

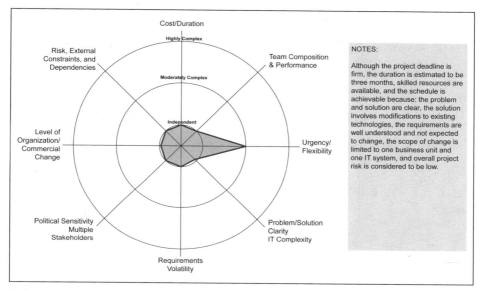

FIGURE 6-1. Example of Independent Project

Highly Complex	Moderately Complex	Independent
Level of change = large-scale enterprise impacts *or* Both the problem and the solution are difficult to define or understand, and the solution is difficult to achieve. The solution is likely to use unproven technologies. *or* Four or more categories in the "highly complex" column	Two or more categories in the "moderately complex" column *or* One category in the "highly complex" column and three or more in the "moderately complex" column	No more than one category in the "moderately complex" column *and* No categories in the "highly complex" column

TABLE 6-2. Project Complexity Formula

As depicted in Figure 6-2, independent projects are usually predictable and respond well to the use of linear project cycles. Some emerging practices can be used with these cycles, most notably critical chain project management (CCPM), a scheduling technique that improves the plan by ". . . ensuring that it is feasible and immune from common cause variation (uncertainty, or statistical variations). It does this by aggregating uncertainty into buffers at the end of activity paths."[1] Advocates of CCPM contend that projects can be completed in record time using this scheduling and control technique. (For a complete discussion of the CCPM technique, see http://www.advanced-projects.com/CCPM/PMJOURN_R8.PDF.)

The following models can be used effectively to manage independent projects:

➤ Waterfall model

➤ Modified waterfall model

➤ Rapid application development (RAD) model

➤ Vee model.

WATERFALL MODEL

The waterfall model, the archetypical project cycle model from which all others are derived, is a highly effective project cycle for short-duration, well-understood projects with stable requirements and virtually no external dependencies. This is the classic systems development life cycle developed by Dr. Win Royce in 1969. Royce intended to provide a repeatable process for the undisciplined software development community. The model has been widely applied to both software and hardware development projects.

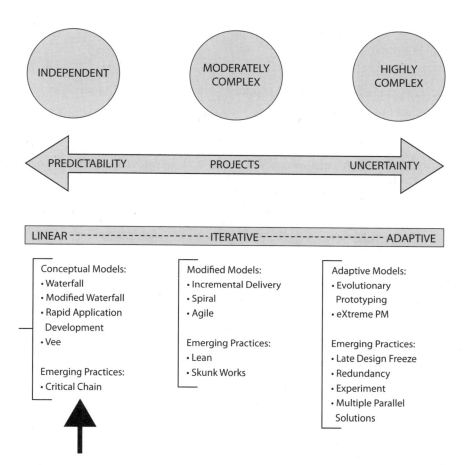

FIGURE 6-2. Independent Projects Mapped to Project Cycle Approaches

The waterfall model is essentially a linear, sequentially based ordering of activities that presumes that requirements are fully developed and approved. It also assumes that events affecting the project are predictable, tools and activities are well-understood, and as a rule, once a phase is complete, it will not be revisited. Development is seen as flowing steadily downward (like a waterfall) through the phases of the model. The "big design up front" approach is often associated with the waterfall model. This approach assumes that the solution design is completed and perfected before construction of the solution is started.

The strengths of the waterfall model are that it lays out the steps for development and stresses the importance of requirements. Its limitations are that projects rarely follow a sequential flow, and clients usually find it difficult to state all requirements fully early in the project. Changes to requirements that involve a change to the scope of the solution can have major impacts on the project schedule and budget, potentially leading to a troubled project. Figure 6-3 depicts the classic waterfall model approach to managing a project.

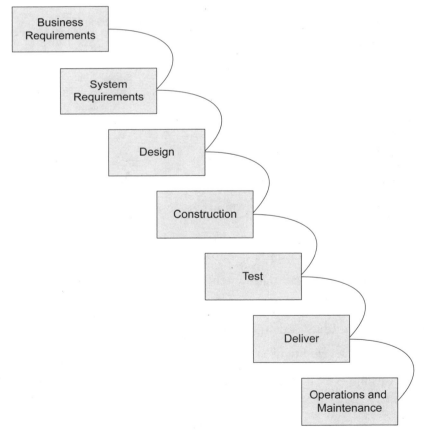

FIGURE 6-3. Waterfall Model

MODIFIED WATERFALL MODEL

The modified waterfall model uses identical phases as the waterfall model, but introduces flexibility by overlapping phases if needed and even splitting the project into subprojects after design is complete. The strength of this approach is that it allows implementation of components of the solution to add value earlier. Its weaknesses are that milestones may be more ambiguous, miscommunication may occur, and unidentified dependencies may create unforeseen problems.[2] Figure 6-4 depicts the modified waterfall model.

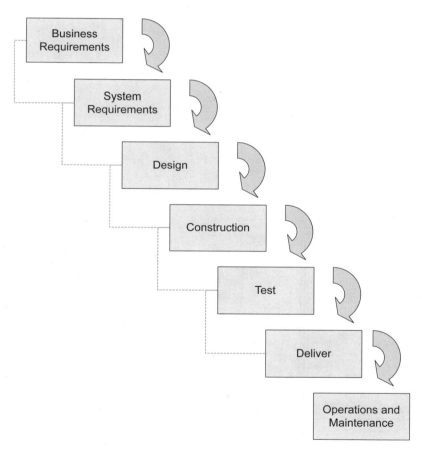

FIGURE 6-4.   Modified Waterfall Model

RAPID APPLICATION DEVELOPMENT MODEL

If requirements are understood and scope is contained, the RAD model allows for a greatly abbreviated development timeline compared to the waterfall model. This component-based approach allows for incremental testing and defect repair—and therefore significantly reduced risk—compared to single, comprehensive delivery. RAD can be costly, however, if requirements aren't well-defined, which creates a high risk of requirements defects, or if the design is not sound, which creates a high risk of integration issues. Figure 6-5 depicts the RAD model.

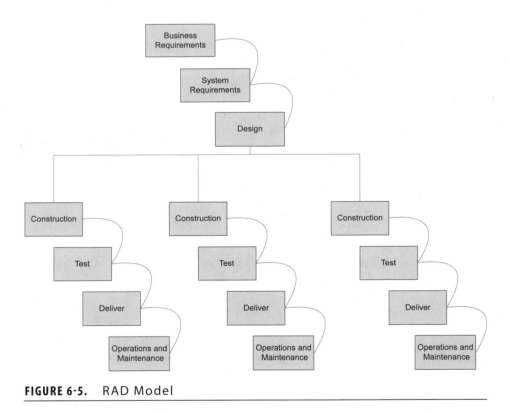

FIGURE 6-5.   RAD Model

VEE MODEL

The Vee model, developed by NASA to manage system engineering projects, is often used for projects once the basic system requirements are firm and system design decisions have been made. The Vee model accounts for the relationships between decomposition, integration, and verification. Integration and verification of subcomponents are planned early. The Vee model assumes the solution will be a closed system, i.e., self-contained and not influenced by its external environment. Accordingly, the system is decomposable, linear, and predictable.[3]

The Vee model involves progressively elaborating requirements, decomposing them for the system into segments, elements, subsystems, and finally components (the left side of the Vee), while defining the approach to integration, verification, and validation (the right side of the Vee) at every decomposition level. Then, integration builds components into subsystems, elements, segments, and finally the system.[4]

The Vee model assumes that the requirements and testing processes, elicited through various business analysis techniques, are known before building begins. In essence, the Vee model adds a vertical dimension to the waterfall model, altering the waterfall shape into a "V." At the base of the Vee is the component build. Components of the system are developed in isolation, and each component produces part of the solution; functionality is gradually integrated into subsequent components.

Unfortunately, this approach does not scale up when addressing large, complex information-age projects because it assumes that a solution will operate in a steady state with static patterns versus flexible solutions that evolve and adapt to their changing environment. Solutions today must be "robust enough to withstand or flexible enough to bend and recover from constant change."[5] Figure 6-6 depicts the classic Vee model.

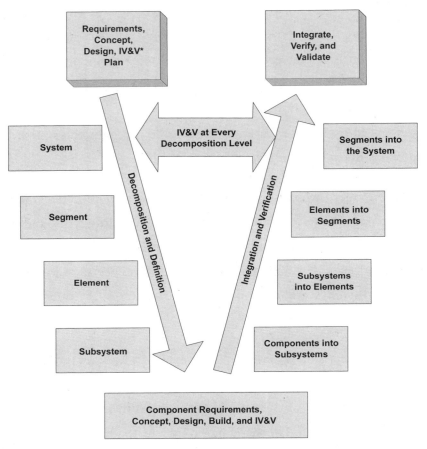

FIGURE 6-6. Vee Model

Well-understood, straightforward projects respond well to linear approaches to project management. When managing independent projects, consider the following project cycle models:

• The waterfall model for well-understood, predictable projects

- The modified waterfall model when implementation of solution components is needed to add value earlier than waiting for the full solution
- The RAD model when the need to deliver the new business solution is urgent
- The Vee model when planning integration and verification of subcomponents early in the project.

NOTES

1. Larry P. Leach, "Critical Chain Project Management Improves Project Performance," Advanced Projects Institute (2000). Online at http://www.advanced-projects.com/CCPM/PMJOURN_R8.PDF (accessed March 2008).
2. Business eSolutions, "Project Lifecycle Models: How They Differ and When to Use Them." Online at http://www.business-esolutions.com/islm.htm#modifiedwaterfall (accessed January 2008).
3. Linda J. Vandergriff, "Complex Venture Acquisition," Complexity Conference White Paper (2006), 6.
4. Hal Mooz, Kevin Forsberg, and Howard Cotterman, *Communicating Project Management* (Hoboken, NJ: John Wiley & Sons, 2003), 334.
5. Linda J. Vandergriff, "Complex Venture Acquisition," Complexity Conference White Paper (2006), 5.

CHAPTER 7

Appropriate Project Cycles for Moderately Complex Projects

As depicted in the *Project Complexity Model,* moderately complex projects are longer in duration (three to six months) than independent projects and they are staffed with adequate project leadership and both internal and external team members (five to ten team members) who use semiformal PM methods and who have a track record of developing fairly reliable estimates. Scope is defined and agreed to, and the schedule and budget have some flexibility.

In moderately complex projects, the business objective is defined, basic requirements are understood but are expected to change, and either the solution is difficult to achieve or the technology is unproven. While executive support is adequate, two or three stakeholder groups are involved and the project has external political implications. The organizational change impacts two or three business units, business processes, and IT systems undergoing maintenance or enhancement. The IT environment is also moderately complex. Some new or unfamiliar regulatory requirements must be met, but the exposure level is acceptable. Table 7-1 presents the profile of a moderately complex project.

Complexity Dimensions	Moderately Complex Project Profile
Time/Cost	3–6 months $250K–750K
Team Size	5–10 team members
Team Composition and Performance	• Competent project leadership • Team staffed with internal and external resources; internal staff has worked together in the past and has track record of reliable estimates • Contract for external resources is straightforward; contractor performance is known • Semi-formal methodology with QA/QC processes defined
Urgency and Flexibility of Cost, Time, and Scope	• Schedule, budget, and scope can undergo minor variations, but deadlines are firm • Achievable scope and milestones
Clarity of Problem, Opportunity, and Solution	• Defined business objectives • Problem or opportunity is partially defined • Solution is partially defined
Requirements Volatility and Risk	• Adequate customer/user support • Basic requirements are understood but are expected to change • Moderately complex functionality
Strategic Importance, Political Implications, Multiple Stakeholders	• Adequate executive support • Some direct impact on mission • Minor political implications • 2–3 stakeholder groups • Challenging communication and coordination effort
Level of Organizational Change	• Impacts 2–3 somewhat familiar business units, processes, and IT systems
Level of Commercial Change	• Enhancements to existing commercial practices
Risks, Dependencies, and External Constraints	• Considered moderate risk • Some project objectives are dependent on external factors • Challenging integration effort • Some new regulatory requirements • Acceptable exposure
Level of IT Complexity	• Solution is difficult to achieve or technology is proven but new to the organization • IT complexity and legacy integration are moderate

TABLE 7-1. Profile of a Moderately Complex Project

In the example presented in Figure 7-1, one dimension of the project falls in the "Highly Complex" area (Urgency/Flexibility) and the rest fall within the "Moderately Complex" area. Our *Project Complexity Formula* (reproduced here as Table 7-2) tells us that this project should be managed as a moderately complex project.

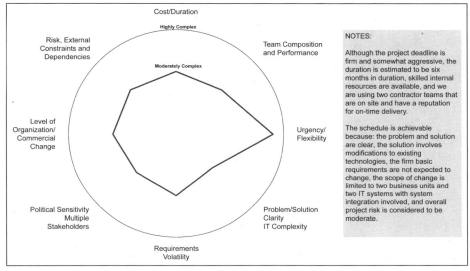

FIGURE 7-1. Example of Moderately Complex Project

Highly Complex	Moderately Complex	Independent
Level of change = large-scale enterprise impacts *or* Both the problem and the solution are difficult to define or understand, and the solution is difficult to achieve. The solution is likely to use unproven technologies. *or* Four or more categories in the "highly complex" column	Two or more categories in the "moderately complex" column *or* One category in the "highly complex" column and three or more in the "moderately complex" column	No more than one category in the "moderately complex" column *and* No categories in the "highly complex" column

TABLE 7-2. Project Complexity Formula

As projects become complex, they also become unpredictable. Recognizing that conventional, linear approaches are not likely to be effective, we need to look for iterative models that allow us to control the unpredictability and uncertainties. Mark Fowler is a strong proponent of iterative development.

MARK FOWLER
The New Methodology[1]

We need an honest feedback mechanism which can accurately tell us what the situation is at frequent intervals. The key to this feedback is iterative development. Iterative development has been around for a while under many names: incremental, evolutionary, staged, spiral . . . lots of names. The key to iterative development is to frequently produce working versions of the final system that have a subset of the required features. These working systems are short on functionality, but should otherwise be faithful to the demands of the final system. They should be fully integrated and as carefully tested as a final delivery.

The point of this is that there is nothing like a tested, integrated system for bringing a forceful dose of reality into any project. Documents can hide all sorts of flaws. Untested code can hide plenty of flaws. But when people actually sit in front of a system and work with it, then flaws become truly apparent: both in terms of bugs and in terms of misunderstood requirements.

Fowler notes that in linear, plan-based models, performance is measured against conformance to the plan. The uncertainties involved make it difficult to determine when the plan no longer represents reality. In contrast, in an iterative environment, the plan is reviewed and reworked at the end of each iteration, incorporating lessons learned from the prior iteration. This approach allows problems with the project schedule to surface early.

As indicated in Figure 7-2, Moderately Complex Projects Mapped to Project Cycle Approaches, iterative approaches become more important as uncertainties increase. Iterative models may also make use of management practices such as:

➤ *Lean:* a philosophy adopted from the world of manufacturing that uses multiskilled teams, emphasizes minimization in time and resources to achieve project objectives, and simplifies processes and methods, with the goal of eliminating non–value-added activities

➤ *Skunk works:* semi-autonomous project teams separated from the workings of the larger organization that work on critical, time-sensitive, complex, and sometimes secret projects.

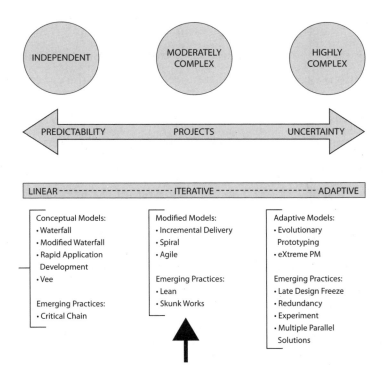

FIGURE 7-2. Moderately Complex Projects Mapped to Project Cycle Approaches

Several iterative models are appropriate as projects become more complex:

➤ Incremental delivery model

➤ Spiral model

➤ Agile model.

INCREMENTAL DELIVERY MODEL

Also referred to as staged delivery and evolutionary delivery, the incremental delivery model delivers valuable increments of functionality—parts of the solution—to the customer earlier than the approach of delivering the full solution at the end of the project (often referred to as "big bang" implementation). This model allows for implementation of the solution incrementally, capitalizing on experience and learnings from the results of prior versions. As the iterations of a cycle build, refine, and review, the correct solution gradually emerges.

Using an incremental delivery model, the project is divided into phases, or iterations, with clear objectives culminating in a project decision gate, where progress and risk are reviewed and plans are set for the next phase. The first phase is typically an effort to define basic requirements and experiment with solution design options aimed at resolving uncertainties about the feasibility of technical options. This first phase may be followed by a series of prototyping iterations designed to bring the solution into view.

Once the solution design is relatively firm, functions are prioritized based on risk, business value, and dependencies between each incremental delivery; once high-risk areas are resolved, the goal is to deliver the highest value components first. Additional parts of the solution are deployed until the complete solution is formulated. This approach can be quite effective, but careful planning is required to develop a viable release schedule. Unforeseen dependencies between the increments can cause rework.

A major difference between the linear approaches (the waterfall and Vee models) relates to scope changes. In the linear models, scope changes are not expected or encouraged. In the incremental model, customers operate the initial releases in a production environment and have the opportunity to recommend improvements to requirements. Figure 7-3 depicts the incremental delivery model.

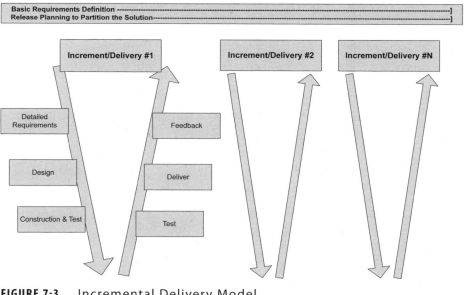

FIGURE 7-3. Incremental Delivery Model

SPIRAL MODEL

The development model that also applies to moderately complex projects is the spiral model developed by Dr. Barry Boehm in 1980. This model focuses on requirements, feasibility, and risk; once these are resolved, teams often transition to the traditional waterfall or Vee model.

The spiral model is often described as an iterative waterfall approach used to encourage customer and stakeholder involvement in risk resolution early in the project. This approach is similar to the prototyping model in that it breaks the project into risk-reduction iterations, each of which addresses a major risk. After all major risks have been addressed, the spiral model terminates as an iterative, adaptive approach and may transition into any other appropriate model. Figure 7-4 depicts the spiral model.

Since early iterations of the project are the cheapest, the spiral model approach enables the project team to address the highest risks at the lowest total cost. This approach ensures that as costs increase, risks decrease. The spiral model approach is quite effective, but skilled management is required to pull it off. Typical steps include:[2]

1. Determine objectives, alternatives, and constraints

2. Identify and resolve risks

3. Evaluate alternatives

4. Develop the deliverables for that iteration and verify that they are correct

5. Plan the next iteration

6. Commit to an approach for the next iteration.

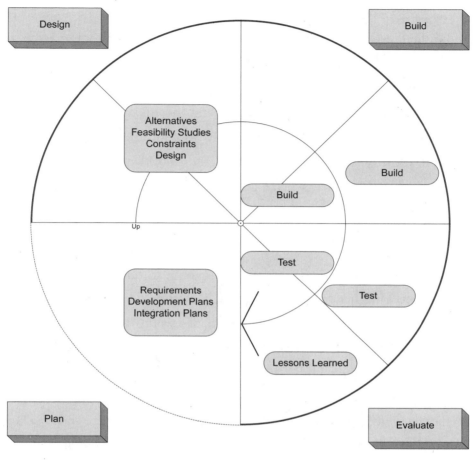

FIGURE 7-4. Spiral Model

AGILE MODEL

"Agility is the ability to both create and respond to change in order to profit in a turbulent business environment. Agility is the ability to balance flexibility and stability."

—JIM HIGHSMITH, CONSULTANT, AUTHOR,
LEADER IN AGILE PROJECT MANAGEMENT

The agile movement is flourishing because requirements are so volatile and difficult to define. The relatively new agile methods attempt to arrive at a compromise between too much and not enough process. The agile model is often used when the business objectives and solution are unknown or not clearly defined. It uses a highly iterative and incremental process whereby developers and project stakeholders actively work together to understand the domain, identify what needs to be built, and prioritize functionality.[3] The agile model is appropriate when a great deal of experimentation is required to develop the optimal solution.

Over the past few years, interest in agile (a.k.a. "lightweight") methodologies has been growing. Described as an approach to rid IT development of burdensome bureaucracy[4] (or alternatively, a "license to hack"), agile methodologies have generated interest throughout the IT world. The emphasis in agile methods differs substantially from the emphasis in traditional, more "heavyweight" engineering methods. The most notable difference is that they are less document-oriented, requiring less documentation for a given task. When agile methods are used for software development, they often use source code as a key part of documentation. Two additional, fundamental distinctions are that:[5]

> *Agile methods are adaptive rather than predictive.* Engineering methods plan out a large part of the solution in great detail and then manage changes throughout the project. Agile methods seek to adapt and thrive on change.

> *Agile methods are people-oriented rather than process-oriented.* The goal of engineering methods is to define a process that is repeatable and independent of the development team. Agile methods focus on the skill of the development team, trying to make the process support the team more effectively in its work.

Much like the early stages of a research and development project, agile methods are used when project value is clear (even if the business objectives are unclear); the customer participates throughout the project; experts (designers, developers, business visionaries, project manager, and business analyst) are co-located; incremental feature-driven development is possible; and visual documentation (cards on the wall versus formal documentation) is acceptable. The agile model involves significant risk, however, because the project often has no fixed budget or timeline—these are impossible to determine because there is no clear goal and solution. Figure 7-5 depicts the agile model.

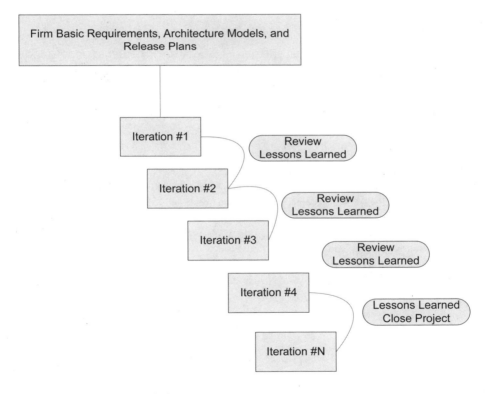

FIGURE 7-5. Agile Model

Moderately complex projects require a more iterative approach, providing lots of opportunity to obtain feedback, determine lessons learned, and refine plans moving forward. Several models can be effective for managing moderately complex projects:

- The incremental delivery model, similar to the modified waterfall model, is used when the project deploys valuable increments of functionality—parts of the solution—to the customer earlier than delivering the full solution at the end of the project.
- The spiral model encourages customer and stakeholder involvement in risk resolution early in the project.
- The agile model uses a highly iterative and incremental process whereby developers and project stakeholders actively work together to understand the domain, identify what needs to be built, and prioritize functionality.

NOTES

1. Mark Fowler, "The New Methodology" (2003). Online at http://www.martinfowler.com/articles/newMethodology.html (accessed March 2008).
2. Business eSolutions, "Project Lifecycle Models: How They Differ and When to Use Them." Online at http://www.business-esolutions.com/islm.htm#modifiedwaterfall (accessed January 2008).
3. Scott W. Ambler, "Agile Analysis." Online at http://www.agilemodeling.com/essays/agileAnalysis.htm (accessed January 2008).
4. Mark Fowler, "The New Methodology" (2003). Online at http://www.martinfowler.com/articles/newMethodology.html (accessed March 2008).
5. Ibid.

CHAPTER 8
Appropriate Project Cycles for Highly Complex Projects

"Welcome a certain amount of complexity and churn because it creates a chemical reaction that jars creative thinking."

—COLLEEN YOUNG, VP AND DISTINGUISHED ANALYST AND IT ADVISER, GARTNER

As depicted in the *Project Complexity Model,* highly complex projects are typically designed to bring about large-scale, enterprise-wide change, and both the problem and the solution may be difficult to define, understand, or achieve. In addition, they are likely to be long in duration (more than six months) and may be staffed with inadequately seasoned project leadership and more than ten internal and external team members who use differing project management methods. The team on a highly complex project may not have worked together in the past, so it has no track record of performance. The project scope and schedule are both overambitious, with the schedule having extended milestones and a fixed deadline. Budget, scope, and quality have little or no room for flexibility. The business objective is unclear, and basic requirements are poorly understood and are expected to change. The solution requires groundbreaking innovation using immature and complex technologies, and the IT environment is highly complex.

Executive support for a highly complex project may not be adequate, and overall project success may depend largely on external constraints or dependencies. Multiple stakeholder groups are involved and the project has political implications. Commercial practices may need to undergo groundbreaking innovation. The change brought about by the project has impacts across the enterprise, affecting many dissimilar critical business processes and IT systems. New or unfamiliar regulatory requirements may bring significant exposure. Table 8-1 presents a profile of a highly complex project.

Complexity Dimensions	Highly Complex Project Profile
Time/Cost	> 6 months > $750K
Team Size	> 10 team members
Team Composition and Performance	• Project manager inexperienced in leading complex projects • Complex team structure of varying competencies (e.g., contractor, virtual, culturally diverse, outsourced) • Complex contracts; contractor performance unknown • Diverse methodologies
Urgency and Flexibility of Cost, Time, and Scope	• Over-ambitious schedule and scope • Deadline is aggressive, fixed, and cannot be changed • Budget, scope, and quality have no room for flexibility
Clarity of Problem, Opportunity, and Solution	• Unclear business objectives • Problem or opportunity is ambiguous and undefined • Solution is difficult to define
Requirements Volatility and Risk	• Inadequate customer/user support • Requirements are poorly understood, volatile, and largely undefined • Highly complex functionality
Strategic Importance, Political Implications, Multiple Stakeholders	• Mixed/inadequate executive support • Impact on core mission • Major political implications • Visible at highest levels of the organization • Multiple stakeholder groups with conflicting expectations

Complexity Dimensions	Highly Complex Project Profile
Level of Organizational Change	• Large-scale organizational change that impacts the enterprise • Spans functional groups or agencies • Shifts or transforms the organization • Impacts many business processes and IT systems
Level of Commercial Change	• Groundbreaking commercial practices
Risks, Dependencies, and External Constraints	• Considered high risk • Overall project success depends largely on external factors • Significant integration required • Highly regulated or novel sector • Significant exposure
Level of IT Complexity	• Solution requires groundbreaking innovation • Solution is likely to use immature, unproven, or complex technologies provided by outside vendors • IT complexity and legacy integration are high

TABLE 8-1.   Profile of a Highly Complex Project

In Figure 8-1, an example of a highly complex project, we see that multiple dimensions fall in the "Highly Complex" column. Our Project Complexity Formula (reproduced here as Table 8-2) tells us that a project with these characteristics should be managed as a highly complex project.

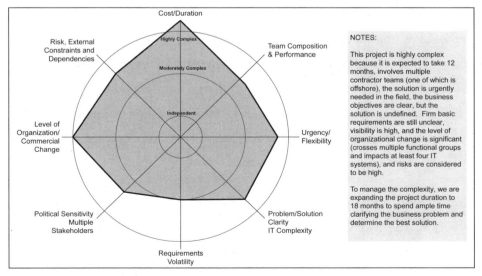

FIGURE 8-1.   Example of Highly Complex Project

Highly Complex	Moderately Complex	Independent
Level of change = large-scale enterprise impacts *or* Both the problem and the solution are difficult to define or understand, and the solution is difficult to achieve. The solution is likely to use unproven technologies. *or* Four or more categories in the "highly complex" column	Two or more categories in the "moderately complex" column *or* One category in the "highly complex" column and three or more in the "moderately complex" column	No more than one category in the "moderately complex" column *and* No categories in the "highly complex" column

TABLE 8-2. Project Complexity Formula

Because complex projects are by their very nature unpredictable, it is imperative that the project team keep its options open as long as possible, building those options into the project approach. This adaptive approach requires that considerable time be dedicated to researching and studying the business problem or opportunity; conducting competitive, technological, and benchmark studies; defining dependencies and interrelationships; and identifying potential options to meet the business need or solve the business problem. In addition, the team experiments with alternative solutions and analyzes the economic, technical, operational, cultural, and legal feasibility of each until it becomes clear which solution option has the highest probability of success. When the opportunity is unclear and the solution is unknown, traditional linear approaches simply will not work.

In highly complex projects, it is important to separate design from construction. The goal is to use expert resources and allow them to spend enough time experimenting before they make design decisions; the construction activities will thereby become much more predictable. Linear methods will likely be appropriate during the construction phase of the project.

Models for adaptive project management are still emerging. We suggest two that are designed to provide iterative learning experiences, adapt and evolve as more is learned, examine and experiment to determine solution design viability, and delay decision-making as long as possible (that is, until the *last responsible moment,* the point at which further delays will put the project at risk): the evolutionary prototyping model and the eXtreme project management model (Figure 8-2). These models employ several contemporary management practices, such as late design freeze, built-in redundancy, lots of experimentation, and designing and building prototypes for multiple parallel solutions.

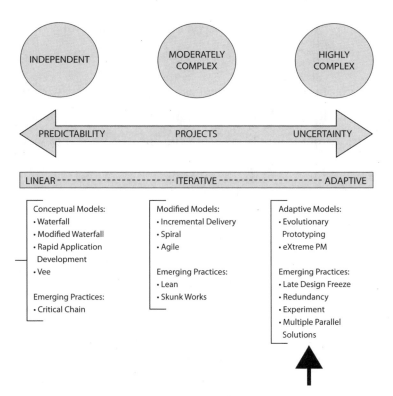

FIGURE 8-2. Highly Complex Projects Mapped to Project Cycle Approaches

EVOLUTIONARY PROTOTYPING MODEL

"The best representation of a complex system is the system itself."
—GÖKTUĞ MORÇÖL, ASSOCIATE PROFESSOR, PUBLIC AFFAIRS
PENN STATE UNIVERSITY

The "keep-our-options-open" approach often involves rapid prototyping—a fast build of a solution component to prove that an idea is feasible—which is typically used for high-risk components, requirements understanding, or proof of a concept.

Evolutionary prototyping is quite effective for multiple iterations of requirements elicitation, analysis, and solution design. Iteration is the best defense against uncertainty because with each iteration the technical and business experts examine the prototype and provide learnings that are built into the next iteration.

The strength of prototyping is that customers work closely with the project team, providing feedback on each iteration. If requirements are unclear and highly volatile, prototyping helps bring the business need into view.[1] Figure 8-3 depicts the rapid prototyping model.

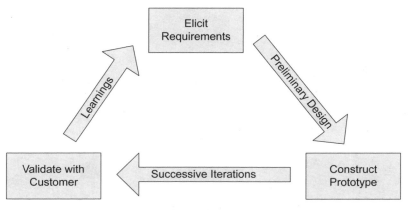

FIGURE 8-3. Rapid Prototyping Model

eXtreme PROJECT MANAGEMENT MODEL

"An extreme project is a complex, high-speed, self-correcting venture during which people interact in search of a desirable result under conditions of high uncertainty, high change, and high stress."

—DOUG DECARLO, AUTHOR AND LECTURER

The eXtreme project management model was developed by Doug De-Carlo and is fully defined in his book, *eXtreme Project Management: Using Leadership, Principles, and Tools to Deliver Value in the Face of Volatility.*[2] The model is designed to be used when a great deal of change is expected during the project, speed is of the essence, and uncertainty and ambiguity exist. Pharmaceutical research for a groundbreaking drug, new product development for a pioneering invention, and major business change efforts are examples of extreme projects.

The eXtreme project management model consists of a set of principles, values, questions, and success factors that can be applied effectively to highly complex projects. These elements are outlined in Table 8-3.

Principles *Accelerators for unleashing motivation and innovation*	Shared Values *For building trust and confidence*	Business Questions *For ensuring customers receive value early and often*	Critical Success Factors

• Change is your friend
• People want to make a difference
• People support what they create
• Simplicity wins
	• Client collaboration
	• People first
	• Clarity of purpose
	• Honest communication
	• Results orientation
	• Fast failures
	• Early value
	• Visibility
	• Quality of life
	• Courage
		• Who needs what and why?
		• What will it take to do it?
		• Can we get what it takes?
		• Is it worth it?
			• Self-mastery
			• Leadership by commitment
			• Flexible project model
			   –Initiate
			   –Speculate
			   –Innovate
			   –Re-evaluate
			   –Disseminate
			• Real-time communication
			• Agile organization

TABLE 8-3. Elements of the eXtreme Project Management Model

This approach consists of a number of short, experimental iterations designed to determine project goals and identify the most viable solution. As in the agile model, eXtreme project management requires that the customer be involved every step of the way until the solution emerges—a practice that involves many iterations. Like the spiral model, the eXtreme model terminates after the solution is found (or when the sponsor is unwilling to fund any more research); the project team then transitions to one of the other appropriate models.

DeCarlo depicts eXtreme project management as a squiggly line that shows the project from start to finish, demonstrating the open, elastic approach that is required (see Figure 8-4). The focus is on the art of project management versus the more scientific and technical scheduling and planning. eXtreme project management is sometimes also called radical project management or adaptive project management. Some equate it to agile project management.

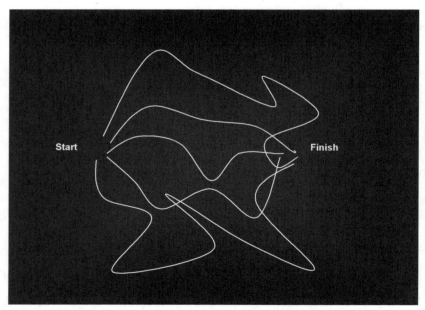

FIGURE 8-4. Open Approach of eXtreme Project Management Model

Since complex projects are by their very nature unpredictable, it is important for the project team to keep its options open, even building options into the project approach. Two models that can be effective for managing highly complex projects are:

- The rapid prototyping model, which is used when multiple iterations of requirements elicitation, analysis, and solution design are needed to bring about clarity.
- The eXtreme project management model, which is used when a number of short iterations are undertaken to determine project goals and the most viable solution.

NOTES

1. Business eSolutions, "Project Lifecycle Models: How They Differ and When to Use Them." Online at http://www.business-esolutions.com/islm.htm#modifiedwaterfall (accessed January 2008).
2. Doug DeCarlo, *eXtreme Project Management: Using Leadership, Principles, and Tools to Deliver Value in the Face of Volatility* (San Francisco: Jossey-Bass, 2004).

CONCLUSION TO PART III

Pay close attention to the project cycle that is used on your complex projects. As we have learned, one size does not fit all. Sophisticated project cycles have emerged to manage the complexities that arise on projects. Use the *Project Complexity Model* to inform the project leadership team about the project's profile and complexity dimensions. Armed with this information, the team will be well-equipped to determine the appropriate project cycle to use.

PART IV

Managing the Dimensions of Project Complexity

"Traditional management techniques are based on a desire to structure and simplify in order to 'stabilise' complex situations. Yet, sometimes, startling and creative solutions can emerge from that very instability. The trick is to know when 'sticking to the knitting' will be the most productive approach, and when moving a project to the 'edge of chaos' might deliver unexpected performance."

—HUGH CRAIL, PA CONSULTING

Taking one industry as an example, an examination of initiatives that are underway in financial services organizations around the globe reveals that most of the big firms are actively acquiring smaller companies, while pursuing at least these three interrelated goals:[1]

➤ Developing synergies from operations and IT infrastructures to reduce costs across the supply chain

➤ Increasing cross-selling of their own and their business partners' products

➤ Enabling customers to do business with the company through whichever channel they find most convenient.

These critical changes all need to be developed and implemented concurrently, without disruption to the business—in essence, "while the plane is in the air." Countless interdependencies among the three initiatives must be understood and managed. Clearly, a new framework for managing multiple complex business initiatives is needed.

In this part we examine the nature of the dimensions of project complexity presented in the *Project Complexity Model* introduced in Chapter 3 and consider the impacts those complexity dimensions may have on various aspects of a business. We then offer an array of managerial options for your project leadership team to consider.

Complex project management is sensible chaos: the right balance betweens plans (static) and process (dynamic). Some of the managerial options we recommend are conventional project management techniques, and some are definitely on the edge of chaos. We demonstrate how complexity thinking can be applied to manage changes and uncertainties while fostering creativity and innovation. We have included the *CHAOS Ten Recipe for Project Success* elements identified by the Standish Group as appropriate.

We describe the techniques we recommend for dealing with each dimension of complexity in sufficient detail to enable your project leadership team to consider all aspects and implications of the technique. We focus on the following dimensions of project complexity:

➤ In Chapter 9 we examine the complexities of large, long-duration projects.

➤ In Chapter 10 we look at the complexities of large, dispersed, culturally diverse project teams.

➤ In Chapter 11 we examine the complexities of highly innovative, urgent projects with aggressive scopes and schedules.

➤ In Chapter 12 we examine the complexities caused by ambiguous business problems, opportunities, and solutions.

➤ In Chapter 13 we explore the complexities that stem from poorly understood, volatile requirements.

➤ In Chapter 14 we look at the complexities involved in highly visible strategic projects, which are often politically sensitive.

➤ In Chapter 15 we study the challenges of leading complex, large-scale change initiatives.

➤ In Chapter 16 we examine the risks involved in managing projects with significant dependencies and external constraints.

➤ In Chapter 17 we explore the challenges of managing projects with a high level of IT complexity.

NOTE

1.   Hugh Crail, "Putting Complexity Thinking into Practice: Viewpoint on Complexity," PA Consulting Services Limited (2005). Online at http://www.paconsulting.com/insights/managing_complex_projects/ (accessed February 2008).

CHAPTER 9

Applying Complexity Thinking to Large, Long-Duration Projects

	Independent	Moderately Complex	Highly Complex
Time/Cost	< 3 months < $250K	3–6 months $250K–750K	> 6 months > $750K
Team Size	3–4 team members	5–10 team members	> 10 team members

I n this chapter we first explore the nature of project complexity on large, long-duration projects, which often span multiple years. We then recommend techniques for you to consider in leading your team to manage the project and deliver the most innovative solution.

WHAT MAKES LARGE, LONG-DURATION PROJECTS COMPLEX?

Of the various elements that combine to make long-duration projects complex, the most significant is the inevitable changes that will occur in the business environment, which will necessitate adjustments to virtually all elements of the project approach. Project size matters as well, with research demonstrating that the smaller the team, the greater the likelihood of success. In addition, team fatigue and burnout lead to complex human interactions and unavoidable staff turnover.

CONSTANT CHANGE

History is littered with large, long-duration projects that have failed to deliver (e.g., the Denver Airport, Boston's Big Dig). One of the biggest problems with long-term projects is that so many unforeseeable things can happen. No matter how hard we try to stabilize requirements, complaining that the customer keeps changing its mind, the fact is, *change happens.* If project teams cannot adapt, these long-duration projects run the risk of working to achieve a business objective that is no longer valid or relevant: The new business solution the team is building simply may not meet current business needs. Dependencies on other projects or external constraints that have been identified and managed may disappear, but new ones will emerge. Because of constant change and uncertainty, long-duration projects in general elicit a lack of confidence in time and cost estimates and often an inability to deliver anything of value.

SIZE MATTERS

The Standish Group's research has identified three key metrics that can predict with a high degree of certainty whether a project will be successful: project size, project duration, and team size. CHAOS research confirms that small projects are more likely to succeed than large projects.[1] However, most business transformation projects are large and long, involving an enormous amount of work. We recommend using an iterative, incremental approach to managing a long-duration project, to limit the dependencies and to structure the solution into small, manageable increments.

TEAM FATIGUE AND STAFF TURNOVER

Contemplate for a moment the trials and tribulations of a four-person crew crowded into a small capsule on a space flight. Long-duration interplanetary flight poses enormous challenges physically, socially, and psychologically. In prolonged space flight, a distinctive group culture will develop and the crew members will need strong coping mechanisms and a high tolerance of enforced social associations. Personality characteristics resilient against social burnout and psychological stress may be as important to a successful mission as the design of the mission vehicle itself. [2]

The situation flight crews find themselves in is not unlike that of project team members placed on a new, long-duration project where the workload is extreme, the project mission is critical, and there is no end in sight. The stress levels caused by forced interactions can elicit a reaction from the nervous system similar to a mild version of the alarm response to danger. When team members are commingled for a prolonged period, they may experience exhaustion that can trigger depression, insomnia, attention deficits, mood instabilities, and even sometimes immune system pressure that results in physical illness. Long-term projects tend to expose our weakest links as our ability to endure extended periods of heavy workload conditions are stretched to the limit.[3]

The human element adds a great deal of complexity to long-duration projects. Human behavior is unpredictable. Team members are dependent on each other for success. Intricate associations develop among team members, adding invisible and unknown dependencies. Likewise, interrelationships develop between team members and stakeholders external to the project team. The informal communication networks and alliances that emerge are unpredictable and unmanageable.

CASE STUDY: LARGE, LONG-DURATION PROJECT
Heathrow Airport, Terminal 5

One of the longest, most drawn out contemporary projects was the effort to build Terminal 5 at Heathrow Airport in London. This 13-year effort is a prime example of a complex, long-duration project involving many complexity dimensions, including an intricate set of contractor teams, multiple stakeholders, high visibility, and numerous external constraints such as building codes and environmental standards.

The proposal for the new terminal was submitted in January 1995 and approved in 2001 after 46 months of public inquiry. Construction finally started in 2002, involving more than 60 contractors. Many commitments made during the early public meetings when little was known about the site were considered fixed and unchangeable, thus imposing costly and time-consuming constraints on the terminal design.

Phase One of the terminal opening ran behind schedule and eventually occurred in March 2008. During the 13-year timeline, the airline and airport businesses changed dramatically, yet the project was unable to adapt and evolve with the industry. For example:[4]

- *Sustainability*—more was learned about the climate, resources, pollution, and noise that needed to be taken into account.
- *Technology*—advancements in software technology, communications, user interfaces, intelligent buildings, and materials during the project life span caused unanticipated changes.

Lessons learned from this project indicate that the flexibility to respond to changes is critical to the success of long-duration projects. This project provides a strong argument for flexibility in decision-making as more is learned during all phases of long-duration projects.

DEALING WITH THE COMPLEXITIES OF LARGE, LONG-DURATION PROJECTS

The complexities of long-duration projects require that special attention be directed to planning and structuring the project, developing and delivering the solution, selecting team members, and sustaining a high-performing team over the long haul.

PLANNING AND STRUCTURING THE PROJECT

Our recommendations for planning and structuring large, long-duration projects include:

➤ Select the appropriate management approach

➤ Progressively elaborate the plan

➤ Use a systematic, reliable approach to estimating

➤ Perform rigorous time and cost management

➤ Use stage-gate management

➤ Conduct rigorous risk management.

Select the Appropriate Management Approach

Rigorous enterprise analysis should be performed during the pre-project study phase or immediately following project initiation to clarify high-level management issues and help the sponsor, customer, business analyst, architect, and project manager make the appropriate management choices for the project. The project leadership team should determine the specific nature of the business problem, appropriate management approach (e.g., linear, iterative, adaptive), and team structure. The team should work to answer questions like: Is this really a program? Is it a series of modestly scoped, small projects? Something else? Must the project or program deliver a product line, a system of systems? Can the solution be delivered in components?

Especially for long-duration projects, success depends on selecting the management approach best suited to deal with the changes that will inevitably occur. The project leadership team needs to (1) recognize the nature of the problem and solution, (2) understand that the conventional, reductionist systems/software engineering and project management approaches may not work, and then (3) make the right choice of management approaches (e.g., conventional versus adaptive techniques, appropriate project cycles, the best project team structure). Continuous customer and end-user evaluation and feedback should be built into the approach to ensure that the project team delivers what is needed—which often is not what was originally proposed.[5]

Progressively Elaborate the Plan

Progressive elaboration is defined by the *PMBOK® Guide* as a technique for continuously improving and adding detail to the plan as more information becomes available. The goal is for more accurate and complete plans to emerge from the successive iterations of the planning process. Also referred to as *rolling wave planning* and *just-in-time planning,* the detailed plan covers just a few weeks or months, and only high-level milestones are identified for the rest of the project. The plan thus evolves and adapts to changes as they occur.

Instead of trying to plan the entire project, start by scheduling the activities to define *firm basic requirements.*[6] At the same time, begin to plan activities to develop a conceptual design of the solution at a high level, resisting design decisions that will impose constraints. Define the remaining components only at a *milestone* level (the *PMBOK® Guide* defines a milestone as a significant point or event in the project), based on the project cycle you have selected (as described in Part III). Sometimes it is advisable to set up a proof-of-concept pilot project to build small-scale prototype components of the solution and plan for interim decision points before launching into the full-blown project. Other times, you should separate a high-risk component of the full solution (e.g., the baggage system for Denver International Airport, which caused huge delays and cost overruns) and treat it very differently from the rest of the project.[7]

After basic requirements are understood and considered firm, and the team has an initial concept of what the solution will be, you will be able to plan the design, construction, and test activities in more detail. This approach makes it possible to request funding and the resources needed in increments instead of all at once.

RECIPE FOR PROJECT SUCCESS: THE CHAOS TEN
The Standish Group International, Inc. 2001
#7: Firm Basic Requirements[8]

The key to understanding this item is the word "basic," which refers to base-level requirements. The objective is to create a minimal, obtainable base level of requirements, and then to develop features for those base requirements that will minimize the effect of changes. Delivering minimal features allows users and executive sponsors to see results quickly. An added benefit is that project managers are better prepared to articulate the needs and priorities of the next phase of the project.

Use a Systematic, Reliable Approach to Estimating

According to the Standish Group, although 28 percent of IT projects are coming in on time and on budget, most of those projects were originally overestimated. In a number of focus groups, "IT executives reported that they first get their best estimates, multiply by two and then add a half. It should not be surprising, therefore, that the majority of these successful projects were already 150% over budget before they began."[9] The report goes on to state the obvious: Reliable estimates are "rare birds" and our current estimating methods for IT projects are outmoded and ineffective.

Nonetheless, we must strive to come up with the best estimate we can. In fact, one precondition to being assigned as manager of a complex project should be a track record of developing reliable estimates. To increase reliability, we recommend using multiple estimating techniques. In addition, educate your project sponsor and other key stakeholders about the fallibility of estimates in general and discuss the reliability they can expect from your specific estimates.

Using progressive elaboration planning techniques, your near-term estimates derived from a detailed schedule should be quite reliable, within +/–10 percent (bottom-up estimates). But for out-phases where detailed planning has not yet occurred and the complete picture has not yet come into view (top-down estimates), it is wise to give a range for your cost and time estimates (e.g., $500K–$750K, four to six months) and a reliability designator (e.g., 75 percent probability).

Without a doubt, early estimates will be highly unreliable, exhibiting a wide range of variability. Numerous uncertainties are involved when building something unique with a team that has not worked together in the past. However, once the project has executed through a few iterations (if using incremental techniques) or through a few project phases (if using linear techniques), you can begin to gauge the speed of progress and adjust your original estimates accordingly. In *Estimation for Agile Projects,* Mike Griffiths presents a thorough discussion of estimating best practices that can be applied to virtually all projects.[10]

A variety of cost estimating techniques can be used. In an uncertain world, involve numerous stakeholders, use multiple techniques to confirm the reliability of your estimates, and document the assumptions and methods you used to come up with them. Use expert judgment and historical information from similar projects to help devise and verify early estimates. It may also be helpful to use industry guidelines to create estimates.

There are two broad categories of estimates, heuristic and parametric:

➤ *Heuristic:* based on expert judgment

　❯ *Top-down estimates,* also referred to as *activity-based estimates*—estimates are calculated using a broad, high-level deliverables list; they involve generating estimates for large units of work.

　❯ *Bottom-up estimates,* also referred to as *task-based estimates*—estimates are calculated using a complete, detailed work breakdown structure (WBS); they involve generating estimates for small units of work. Build a WBS and estimate the time and cost associated with lowest-level activities for near-term project phases.

　❯ *Work distribution estimates*—effort is estimated by major project phase.

　❯ *Comparison* estimates—effort is compared with completed similar project(s) and adjusted for dissimilarities.

➤ *Parametric:* based on calculations

   ❯ *Function point estimates*—estimates are developed for logical business views of components of the solution (e.g., for each function: inputs, outputs, tables, queries, and interfaces).

   ❯ *Use case point estimates*—estimates are developed based on the number of use cases.

RECIPE FOR PROJECT SUCCESS: THE CHAOS TEN
The Standish Group International, Inc. 2001
#9: Reliable Estimates

When developing a systematic approach toward project estimating, it is essential to be realistic. Estimating is just plain hard. Managers must use all their collective knowledge and experience to come up with estimates that reflect the true effort required.[11]

1. Create and maintain accurate estimates and develop a more systematic approach toward project estimating and costing.
2. Know that projects are marathons, so prepare for the long run.
3. Look at ways to make your project more financially attractive.
4. Consider working with a project budget and understand how companies manage their information technology money.
5. Know the elusive financial breakeven point and how that point changes as the project moves forward.
6. Manage change; failure to do so is almost always a major contributor to project failure.
7. Use incentives to finish the project as a way to improve success and reduce failures.

8. Don't be afraid to kill a project and take your lumps and losses.
9. Recognize the benefits of pruning or refactoring your code—cutting out unused or meaningless code.
10. Create a functional pipeline.

Developing good estimates is difficult for a variety of reasons. There is usually intense political pressure to make the estimate what the project sponsor or the organization wants to hear to get the project approved. There is also a psychology to estimating—we are hopelessly optimistic and always think we can do more than is possible. And then there are technical issues; for example, projects involving software development simply defy estimation.

Lev Virine and Michael Trumper offer a few golden rules of estimating that they call "simple remedies":[12]

➤ Never make a wild guess

➤ Collect relevant historical data

➤ Perform reality checks

➤ Conduct an independent assessment.

Perform Rigorous Time and Cost Management

Delivering on schedule is one of the main challenges for a long-duration project, simply because of the enormous amount of work to be accomplished. Implement a rigorous process for tracking progress and controlling output. Track progress to the next milestone scrupulously. Manage the schedule and budget by establishing a project support team to update and maintain the schedule and budget baselines; emphasize to team members that they should bring any issues that put the next milestone in jeopardy to your attention.

Use Stage-Gate Management

Stage-gate management can be used to create opportunities to gather feedback from your customers and your team members on a regular basis. After completing each phase or iteration, conduct informal team-based quality reviews of deliverables. As part of these reviews, determine what worked well and identify opportunities for improvement to the solution development process and team operations. Subsequently, conduct a formal external quality assurance review of major deliverables and incorporate actions to correct defects found in the deliverables that must be resolved before work can proceed. Update the project cost, schedule, and scope baselines for the remaining near-term project phases/iterations, incorporating lessons learned into the plans.

Simultaneously, reexamine the business case to validate that business benefits will be achieved and the investment is still sound. Conduct a formal project review with the project sponsor and other key stakeholders to secure approval to formally launch and expend funds for the next phase/iteration.

Conduct Rigorous Risk Management

Few projects perform adequate risk management. For large, long-duration projects, it is essential to identify risks after each iteration/phase and reexamine risk responses to:

➤ Ensure the risk response plans are managing known risks

➤ Identify new risks and develop risk response plans

➤ Identify new project dependencies and interrelationships and develop dependency management plans.

Chapter 16 focuses on risk management as it relates to the management of complex projects.

CASE STUDY: LARGE, LONG-DURATION PROJECT
Development of Large IT Systems

Of the many challenges facing long-duration IT projects—the absence of deep application domain knowledge, volatile and conflicting requirements, and communication bottlenecks and breakdowns—the most difficult is maintaining a focus on the business strategy. To illustrate this, we have selected the case of a large computer manufacturing company.

The organization established a highly skilled IT development team to design and develop the next generation of supply-chain software to handle all the key business processes involved in acquiring goods from suppliers: requisitioning, purchasing, receiving, inspecting, and invoice processing. The development team spent about two years and millions of dollars developing the new IT system. During that time, the market made a dramatic shift and the company strategy changed from an IT software product provider to an IT professional services provider. The new supply chain system was shelved and the investment in its development was never recovered. Had the team kept a pulse on the business strategy, the project would have been canceled or redirected long before millions of dollars were invested in a product with no customers.

DEVELOPING AND DELIVERING THE SOLUTION

We offer a few suggestions for developing and delivering the solution on large, long-duration projects:

➤ Structure your project to develop and deliver the solution incrementally

➤ Minimize scope

➤ Delay design decisions until the last responsible moment

➤ Use rapid application development

➤ Use lean development techniques.

Structure Your Project to Develop and Deliver the Solution Incrementally

> *"Projects should always be managed by rapid learning cycles because what we are doing is so complex that nobody knows the answer to begin with."*
>
> —T. GILB, SOFTWARE ENGINEER AND AUTHOR

Research has repeatedly demonstrated that short-duration projects are more likely to be successful than prolonged endeavors.[13] However, business transformation projects tend to be long and to involve a mix of complex development efforts, such as business process reengineering, legacy IT system replacement, and the creation of new, innovative business practices that rely heavily on technology.

To increase the probability of project success, structure your project into multiple deployments of small solution components rather than taking the "big bang" implementation approach. As you develop and deliver the solution in increments, incorporate lessons learned from each increment into the next iteration and constantly test for alignment with business objectives. This technique establishes a cycle that builds, refines, and reviews, enabling the correct solution to emerge gradually. The project is divided into phases or iterations with clear objectives that culminate in a project decision gate, where progress and risk are reviewed and plans are set for the next phase. The first phase is typically an effort to define basic requirements and experiment with solution design options aimed at resolving uncertainties about the feasibility of technical options. This phase may be followed by a series of prototyping iterations that gradually bring the solution into view. This technique can be difficult to control, but it is highly effective when properly applied.

The Standish Group *Recipe for Project Success* (Table 9-1) asserts that "success is practically in the oven" when a project follows this recipe. Standish reports that the newest data coming in suggest that it is prudent to further reduce the amount of resources (people, time, and cost) to no more than four people, for no longer than four months, at a cost of less than $500,000. For large, long-duration projects, the only way to get the resources down to this level is to structure the effort into a program comprising multiple projects and to use incremental/iterative solution delivery.

Ingredients	Clear business objective; minimized scope (microprojects with rigorous configuration management); constant communication and collaboration; proven, standard, stable software infrastructure (versus custom code); firm basic requirements; formal methodology; reliable estimates
Mix with	Full-time, co-located core team members (experienced business analyst, project manager, business visionary, architects, and developers) coached by an involved executive project sponsor, involved stakeholders, an iterative development process, and effective decision-making tools (requirements tools, project management tools, design/analysis tools, and modeling tools)
Bake	No longer than six months; no more than six people; at no more than $750,000 (1999) No longer than four months; no more than four people; at no more than $500,000 (2001)

TABLE 9-1. Standish Group Recipe for Success, 2001[14]

Minimize Scope

The motto of 21st century projects is: "Barely sufficient is enough to move on." The more features and functions, the larger the project; as we have discovered, *less is more.*

RECIPE FOR PROJECT SUCCESS: THE CHAOS TEN
The Standish Group International, Inc. 2001
#5: Minimized Scope

Since scope impacts time, or project duration, they are linked. Minimizing scope reduces time and therefore increases a project's chances for success. Build business applications to be lean, mean, and powerful by optimizing scope. "You can never be too thin." Work toward accomplishing the following:[15]

1. Minimize scope to facilitate optimization.
2. Understand the merits of stepping-stones (iterations) and the dangers of milestones.
3. Consider time boxing, which involves setting deadlines and a fixed amount of time in which to complete the project or reach stepping-stones.
4. Examine the rules.
5. Manage expectations by minimizing and optimizing the scope.
6. Make use of low-tech tools, like index cards, to help understand scope.
7. Use role models as guides for both good and bad behavior.
8. Assess the needs of a requirement by its yield or gain (its value).
9. Consider the risk of each requirement.
10. Consider cost, risk, and gain as elements to optimizing scope.

So, how does minimizing scope really work? Initially, deliver a minimum viable subset of the full solution to start adding value for the organization as early as possible. Then, continue to deliver components of the system in short-interval deployments. Limit the dependencies between solution components to reduce the cost of changes. Design the solution to be flexible and agile to allow the customer to respond to changes in the business need, technology, or market conditions.

Delay Design Decisions until the Last Responsible Moment

Flexibility comes from delaying design decisions and the start of major activities for key project drivers (information flows, technical decisions, and business decisions) until the *last responsible moment,* that is, the latest moment possible without compromising cost or schedule. This "keep your options open" approach allows for maximum flexibility.[16]

Use Rapid Application Development

Rapid application development (RAD) is a method of fielding multiple design/build/test/deliver teams to work concurrently. If requirements are understood and scope is contained, RAD allows for a greatly abbreviated development timeline. This component-based approach permits incremental testing and defect repair, significantly reducing risk compared to single, comprehensive delivery. As noted, however, RAD can be costly if (1) requirements aren't well-defined, causing a high risk of requirements defects, or (2) the design is not sound, with a minimal number of well-understood dependencies between increments, which can create a high risk of integration and maintenance issues. Figure 6-5 in Chapter 6 depicts the RAD model.

Use Lean Development Techniques

Even though the project is long and complex, do not be tempted to apply more rigor than necessary. Produce documents and conduct meetings only if they add value to the project. Continually verify that the project is building the minimum viable solution. Keep in mind the motto: "Barely sufficient is enough to move forward."

SELECTING TEAM MEMBERS AND SUSTAINING A HIGH-PERFORMING TEAM

For complex, long-duration projects, it is essential to create and sustain a high-performing team. To accomplish this, the project leader should work to:

➤ Select team members for the long haul

➤ Pay close attention to team health

➤ Share resources.

Chapter 10 offers additional recommendations for leading large teams on complex projects.

Select Team Members for the Long Haul

When selecting team members for a long-duration project, keep in mind the special personality traits and coping skills that are needed. Prolonged forced interaction is simply not for everyone. For key positions, select team members who are resilient against social burnout and psychological stress.

Pay Close Attention to Team Health

Longer projects require different planning and development techniques to sustain momentum for the long haul; they also demand that attention be directed to the physical and emotional stresses on the project team members.

Focusing on the health of the team, making strategic personnel changes at critical junctures to infuse new blood, and providing appropriate team leadership will go a long way in sustaining the team.

As a leader of complex projects, continually build your expertise in leading high-performing teams. As the project drags on and fatigue sets in, examine both team composition and team processes and make adjustments as necessary to maintain continued motivation among team members. Celebrate and reward success at key milestones rather than waiting until the end of a long project. Continually capture lessons learned about how well the team is working together and implement suggested improvements.

Share Resources

On long-duration projects, critical resources may not be fully engaged. When this is the case, "lend" them out to a short-duration effort to give the team members a break, allow them to feel the gratification of completing a task or meeting an objective, and then bring them back to your project refreshed and ready to dive back in.

Large, long-duration projects are hard, *very hard*. Strive to understand what makes these types of projects complex: the constant change bombarding organizations today that the project must adapt to, the sheer size of the solution to be constructed and the resources needed, and the inevitable team stress and fatigue.

Using special techniques to plan and structure the project, develop and deliver the solution, and keep team members motivated for the long haul will help you lead a large, complex, long-duration project. Both conventional and adaptive approaches are needed for large, long-duration projects to be successful (see Table 9-2).

Managing Large, Long-Duration Projects	
Complexities	**Management Approaches**
• Constantly changing: – Business goals – Competitors – Global economy – Partnerships and alliances – Stakeholders – Project boundaries – Business objectives – Scope – Dependencies – Interrelationships • Too large: invisible, unmanageable, unable to identify dependencies and relationships • Team fatigue, leading to unpredictable human behaviors	**Adaptive** • Adopt the appropriate project cycle and PM practices for the situation • Minimize scope • Delay design decision until the last responsible moment. • Use incremental development • Use progressive elaboration and rolling wave planning • Establish a systematic estimating process using multiple estimating methods • Pay close attention to team composition and health. • Use lean techniques • Use RAD development to increase velocity for well-understood components **Conventional** • Perform rigorous time and cost management. • Use stage-gate management • Conduct rigorous risk management • Use a systematic approach to develop reliable estimates

TABLE 9-2. Approaches for Managing Large, Long-Duration Projects

NOTES

1. The Standish Group International, Inc., "CHAOS: A Recipe for Success" (1999), 3.
2. Lara Battles, "Coping with Effects of Enforced Intimacy on Long Duration Space Flight," *Proceedings of the Founding Convention of the Mars Society* (1998). Online at http://www.marssociety.com/portal/TMS_Library/MAR_98_065/library_entry_plain_abstract (accessed January 2008).
3. John A. Putman, "EEG Biofeedback and Its Potential Impact on Long Duration Space Missions," In *On to Mars: Colonizing a New World,* Apogee Books (2001). Online at http://www.marssociety.com/portal/TMS_Library/Putman_2001/?searchterm=iss (accessed January 2008).
4. Robert Lane, Vincent C. Lepardo, and Graham Woodman, "How to Deal with Dynamic Complexity on Large, Long Projects." Online at http://www.pbworld.com/library/technical_papers/pdf/32_HowtoDealwithDynamicComplexity.pdf (accessed January 2008).
5. Linda Vandergriff, "Complex Venture Acquisition," Complexity Conference White Paper (2006).
6. The Standish Group International, Inc., "Extreme Chaos" (2001).
7. Aaron Shenhar and Dov Dvir, *Reinventing Project Management: The Diamond Approach to Successful Growth and Innovation* (Boston: Harvard Business School Press, 2007), 6.
8. The Standish Group International, Inc., "Extreme Chaos" (2001).

9. Ibid.

10. Mike Griffiths, "Estimation for Agile Projects" (2008). Online at http://www.gantthead.com/article.cfm?ID=240044 (accessed February 2008).

11. Jim Johnson, *My Life is Failure: 100 Things You Should Know to be a Successful Project Leader* (West Yarmouth, MA: The Standish Group International, 2006), 12.

12. Lev Virine and Michael Trumper, *Project Decisions: The Art and Science* (Vienna, VA: Management Concepts, 2008), 139–142.

13. The Standish Group International, Inc., "Extreme Chaos" (2001).

14. Ibid.

15. Jim Johnson, *My Life is Failure: 100 Things You Should Know to be a Successful Project Leader* (West Yarmouth, MA: The Standish Group International, 2006), 8.

16. Robert Lane, Vincent C. Lepardo, Graham Woodman, "How to Deal with Dynamic Complexity on Large, Long Projects." Online at http://www.pbworld.com/library/technical_papers/pdf/32_HowtoDealwithDynamicComplexity.pdf (accessed January 2008), 5.

CHAPTER 10
Applying Complexity Thinking to Large, Dispersed, Culturally Diverse Project Teams

"A small group of thoughtful people could change the world.
Indeed, it's the only thing that ever has."

—MARGARET MEAD, ANTHROPOLOGIST

Complexity Dimensions	Project Profile		
	Independent	**Moderately Complex**	**Highly Complex**
Team Composition and Performance	• Strong project leadership • Team staffed internally, has worked together in the past, and has a track record of reliable estimates • Formal, proven PM, BA, and SE methodology with QA and QC processes defined and operational	• Competent project leadership • Team staffed with internal and external resources; internal staff has worked together in the past and has a track record of reliable estimates • Contract for external resources is straightforward; contractor performance is known • Semi-formal methodology with QA/QC processes defined	• Project manager inexperienced in leading complex projects • Complex team structure of varying competencies (e.g., contractor, virtual, culturally diverse, outsourced) • Complex contracts; contractor performance unknown • Diverse methodologies

I n this chapter we first explore the nature of project complexity when managing a large, geographically dispersed, diverse team involving complex contractual agreements and multiple methodologies. We then recommend management techniques for project leaders to consider for managing the complexities of the team while establishing an environment of adaptability, innovation, and creativity.

WHAT MAKES LARGE, DIVERSE PROJECT TEAMS COMPLEX?

Complex projects almost always involve multiple layers and types of teams. Applying the most appropriate practices, tools, and techniques to multiple parties at the right time is in itself a complex endeavor. Successful teams are the result of many elements coming together, including team leadership, structure, composition, culture, location, collaboration, communication, coordination, and evolution.

TEAMS AS COMPLEX ADAPTIVE SYSTEMS

All human groups and organizations are complex adaptive systems; teams are complex adaptive systems within the larger organization (which is also a complex adaptive system). As a project manager of a new, complex project, you cannot predict how your team members will react to each other, to the project requirements, and to their place within the organization.

Team members who have worked together in the past may bring biases or resentments toward one another. Team members who have not yet worked together are likely to reserve judgment and hold back interactions until they learn about each other. This concept, referred to as *interactional uncertainty,*[1] theorizes that if there is uncertainty in a relationship, the participants will tend to withhold information and calculate the effects of sharing information. The project manager must guide the team through the inevitable early stages of team growth toward the certainty that leads to trust. Then, team members can focus their energies on positive interactions.

When working with multiple teams, the project manager faces the additional challenge of integrating interdependent solution components that have been designed and constructed by different teams. Moreover, different teams use dissimilar procedures, practices, and tools, resulting in work products of varying quality and consistency.

THE ART OF TEAM LEADERSHIP

Toward the end of the last century, *Fortune* magazine postulated that project management would be the profession of choice in the coming decades. *Fortune* cited trends toward global initiatives, virtual teams, mergers and acquisitions, downsizing and reengineering, and alliances and partnerships— all linking companies in new ways.

In 1999, the Project Management Institute (PMI) discussed the essential skills needed in the 21st century to optimize the power of teams. PMI found that cross-cultural training and awareness, interpersonal skills, team development and leadership, and language facility are becoming conditions for professional success. To manage 21st century complex project teams, these characteristics are not just nice to have; they are vital.

CASE STUDY: LARGE, GEOGRAPHICALLY DISPERSED, CULTURALLY DIVERSE TEAMS
Hurricane Katrina Response

Hurricane Katrina, the costliest and deadliest hurricane in U.S. history, starkly illustrates the consequences of ineffective management of large teams. Katrina caused devastation along much of the north-central Gulf Coast. The most significant loss of life and property damage occurred in New Orleans, Louisiana, which flooded as the levee system failed. The hurricane itself caused severe destruction, and the storm surge caused further damage along the Gulf Coast. The federal flood protection system in New Orleans failed in more than 50 places and the levees breached, flooding 80 percent of the city and many areas of neighboring parishes for weeks. At least 1,836 people lost their lives in Hurricane Katrina and the subsequent floods. The storm is estimated to have been responsible for $81.2 billion in damage, making it the costliest natural disaster in U.S. history.

Many geographically dispersed and culturally diverse teams were part of efforts to (1) respond to the hurricane disaster, (2) protect the safety of victims, and (3) restore and rebuild the areas destroyed by the hurricane and flooding. These groups included:

- *Federal Emergency Management Agency* (FEMA). FEMA's primary mission is to reduce the loss of life and property and to protect the nation from all hazards, including natural disasters, acts of terrorism, and other man-made disasters, by leading and supporting the nation in a risk-based, comprehensive emergency management system of preparedness, protection, response, recovery, and mitigation. On March 1, 2003, FEMA became part of the U.S. Department of Homeland Security (DHS).

- *Offices of the governors* in the states that were impacted and their emergency preparedness agencies.
- *Offices of the mayors* in the cities that were impacted and their emergency preparedness departments.
- *National Guard* contingents in the states that were impacted.
- *Nongovernmental organizations* (NGOs), including the American Red Cross, Southern Baptist Convention, Salvation Army, Oxfam, Common Ground Collective, Emergency Communities, Habitat for Humanity, Service International, A River of Hope, and many other charitable organizations.

It is no secret that the disaster response and subsequent cleanup effort have been inadequate. The federal, state, and local governments' reactions to the storm were widely criticized. The poor response immediately following the disaster and the inadequate cleanup and restoration were blamed on a number of factors, including:

- Lack of clear roles and responsibilities among the local, state, and federal governments
- Mismanagement and lack of leadership
- Decision-making barriers presented by bureaucracy and protocol
- Loss of most means of communication (e.g., land-based and cellular telephone systems)
- Inadequate logistics capacity to fully support the disaster response.

HOW TO LEAD LARGE, GEOGRAPHICALLY DISPERSED, CULTURALLY DIVERSE PROJECT TEAMS

To lead complex layers of teams, project managers must understand the potential power of teams; team leadership; and team collaboration, communication, and coordination.

TEAM POTENTIAL

Teams are a critical asset used to improve performance in all kinds of organizations. Yet today's business leaders consistently overlook opportunities to exploit their potential, confusing teams with teamwork, empowerment, or participative management.[2] We simply cannot meet 21st century challenges, from business transformation to innovation to global competition, without understanding and leveraging the power and wisdom of teams.

Leverage the Power of Teams

"Teams help ordinary people achieve extraordinary results."
—W.H. Murray, Scottish Himalayan Expedition

It is essential for leaders of complex projects to understand the power of teams. Success stories abound: Motorola surpassed the Japanese in the battle to dominate the cell phone market by using teams as a competitive advantage; 3M uses teams to reach its goal of generating half of each year's revenues from the previous five years' innovations.

High-performing teams are all around us: U.S. Navy Seals, tiger teams established to perform a special mission or tackle a difficult problem, paramedic teams, firefighter teams, surgical teams, symphony orchestras, and professional sports teams. These teams demonstrate their accomplishments, insights, and enthusiasm on a daily basis and are a persuasive testament to the power of teams. Clearly, we must learn how to form, develop, and sustain high-performing teams if we are to deliver on complex projects.

Harness the Wisdom of Teams

> *"None of us is as smart as all of us."*
>
> —KEN BLANCHARD, CONSULTANT, SPEAKER, TRAINER, AUTHOR

For complex problems, a team is much more effective than a single person. Warren Bennis talks about teams as great groups, stating: "The genius of *Great Groups* is that they get remarkable people—strong individual achievers—to work together to get results." Along the way, members of these groups provide support and camaraderie for each other. Bennis describes the defining characteristics of great groups:[3]

- ➤ At the heart of every great group is a shared dream.

- ➤ They manage conflict by abandoning individual egos to the pursuit of the dream.

- ➤ They are protected from the "suits."

- ➤ They have a real or invented enemy.

- ➤ They view themselves as winning underdogs.

- ➤ Members pay a personal price.

- ➤ Great groups make strong leaders.

- ➤ Great groups are the product of meticulous recruiting.

- ➤ Real artists ship (i.e., deliver the goods).

For the project manager who is struggling to understand how to build high-performing teams, a must-read is *The Wisdom of Teams*, by Jon Katzenbach and Douglas Smith.[4] The authors talked with hundreds of people in more than 50 teams in 30 companies to discover what differentiates various levels of team performance, where and how teams work best, and how to enhance their effectiveness. Among their findings are elements of both common and uncommon sense:

➤ Commitment to performance goals and common purpose is more important to team success than team-building.

➤ Opportunities for teams exist in all parts of the organization.

➤ Formal hierarchy is actually good for teams (and vice versa).

➤ Successful team leaders do not fit an ideal profile and are not necessarily the most senior people on the team.

➤ Real teams are the most common characteristic of successful change efforts at all levels.

➤ Top management teams are often difficult to sustain.

➤ Despite the increased number of teams, team performance potential is largely unrecognized and underutilized.

➤ Team "endings" can be as important to manage as team beginnings.

➤ Teams produce a unique blend of performance and personal learning results.

Wisdom lies in recognizing a team's unique potential to deliver results. Project leaders strive to understand the benefits of teams and learn how to optimize team performance by developing individual members, fostering team cohesiveness, and rewarding team results. Katzenbach and Smith argue that teams are the primary building blocks of strong company performance. Project managers at all levels cannot afford to ignore the power and wisdom of teams as we strive to meet the competitive challenges of the 21st century.[5]

TEAM LEADERSHIP

We offer a diverse set of suggestions for exceptional team leadership:

➤ Accept no substitute for experience at the helm

➤ Build a great team

➤ Get the "right stuff" on your team

➤ Establish a great team structure

➤ Empower your team members

➤ Build a culture of discipline

➤ Lead, *don't manage,* contractor teams

➤ Use virtual teams as a strategic advantage

➤ Encourage innovation through edge-of-chaos leadership

➤ Manage agile teams with a light touch.

Accept No Substitute for Experience at the Helm

The need for effective team leadership can no longer be overlooked. Technology, techniques, and tools are not the reason projects fail: Projects fail because of people. Team leadership differs significantly from traditional management, just as teams differ from operational work groups.

As discussed in Part II, complex projects are not for the novice. Complex projects are more often than not charged with bringing about the change needed for the organization to remain competitive; indeed, they are sometimes about the organization's very survival. We need only look at the number of companies that have disappeared to know that the competitive environment is fierce. Insist on securing seasoned, experienced, expert, and influential project managers to lead complex projects.

Because complex projects usually have a large, dispersed, complex team structure, the project manager leads through others more than manages the project. Team leadership is more of an art than a science and is fraught with trial, error, and experience. Expertise in communications, problem-solving, and conflict resolution is essential. Leaders of complex projects derive their power and influence not so much from a position of authority in the organizational hierarchy but as a result of their ability to build relationships. These leaders must be:

➤ Held in high regard

➤ Considered to be experts

➤ Known to have important and relevant information

➤ Well-connected with a powerful network

➤ Considered indispensable.

Project managers of complex projects need to understand the difference between traditional project management and adaptive project management (as discussed in Part II) so that they are able to apply the varied managerial techniques appropriately. They become *situational project leaders* who know the difference between command and control versus collaboration and teamwork—and when to apply each approach for the best results.

> ### RECIPE FOR PROJECT SUCCESS: THE CHAOS TEN
> ## The Standish Group International, Inc. 2001
> ### *#3: Experienced Project Manager*
>
> Ninety-seven percent of successful projects have an experienced project manager at the helm. Project managers must:[6]
>
> 1. Ensure that their projects follow project management fundamentals
> 2. Possess project management skills and an appreciation for what makes projects succeed
> 3. Exhibit leadership qualities
> 4. Make and maintain connections
> 5. Promote both an individual and a collective sense of ownership among the team
> 6. Recognize that members of a project team are inclined to have a stronger commitment if they feel their participation and contributions are valued
> 7. Understand the business
> 8. Be able to pass judgment on issues under consideration and reach a firm decision.

Leaders of large, dispersed, diverse teams must have an understanding of the dynamics of team development and how teams work. Leaders of successful teams develop specialized skills that they use to build and sustain high performance. Traditional managers and technical experts cannot necessarily become effective team leaders without appropriate team leadership training and coaching.

Make a concerted effort to develop team-leadership skills and dedicate efforts to transitioning team members into a cohesive team with shared values, beliefs, and cultural foundation. The best teams are collaborative and share the leadership role, depending on the precise needs of the project at any given time. The situational team leader understands that varying leadership styles are appropriate depending on the different stages of team development. Table 10-1, Five-Stage Team Development Model, presents David Kolb's approach to team leadership, which suggests that the situational team leader seamlessly adapts his or her leadership style as the team evolves.

Development Phase	Team Leader Style
Building	Facilitator
Learning	Mediator
Trusting	Coach
Working	Consultant
Flowing	Collaborator

Source: David C. Kolb, *Team Leadership,* © 1999 by Lore International Institute. Reprinted with permission.

TABLE 10-1.   Five-Stage Team Development Model

Aaron Shenhar, professor of management and founder of the project management program at Stevens Institute of Technology, summarizes the strategic role of the complex project leader as follows:

In the traditional project management world, project managers and teams are typically focused on efficiency, operational performance, and meeting time and budget goals. This approach is mainly process-oriented, where project teams are required to follow a structured process of planning, execution, and control; however, today's dynamic environment, rapid technological change, and global competition require looking at projects in a new way. . . . The new way is much more strategic in nature. It views project managers as leaders, who must deal with the strategic, operational, and human sides of project leadership. They must employ an integrated systems approach in order to achieve strate-gic goals of their projects and maximize the benefits and satisfaction of their stakeholders. In the business world, this means being responsible for business results; in the public sector, it means being responsible for value creation and customer satisfaction.[7]

Build a Great Team

As we strive to build high-performing project teams, it is wise to examine the characteristics of great teams outside the business environment (e.g., professional sports teams, heart transplant teams, special operations teams, paramedic teams, fire fighters). What do they all have in common? High-performing teams are small but mighty—diverse, expert, highly trained, and highly practiced. They invest heavily in honing their skills, and they have a coach (an involved sponsor) who removes barriers to success and is available just down the hall 24/7. In addition, they share a common vision, mission, and objectives, and they are passionate. They are co-located and clearly understand their roles and responsibilities, yet each member can cover for the others if need be.

As complex adaptive social systems, some teams will reach and sustain high performance, continually evolving and adapting. Others might be in this stage on a sporadic basis or in subsets of the team.

Outstanding teams can achieve significantly higher performance, leading to more innovative solutions. However, this superior performance does not come easily: It takes time for a team to develop from a newly formed group into a high-performing team. Decisions are made slowly to allow for input from all valued experts; team decisions are generally much more creative than those made by a single individual. Clearly, organizations need to invest in their teams through training, coaching, and team rewards.

Get the "Right Stuff" on Your Team

When you select team members, do so not only based on their knowledge and skills, but also because they are passionate, strategic thinkers who thrive in a challenging, collaborative environment.

RECIPE FOR PROJECT SUCCESS: THE CHAOS TEN
The Standish Group International, Inc. 2001
#10: Competent Staff

Acquire and support skilled resources and manage them with truthfulness, training, and communication.[8]

1. Determine what you need to consider in evaluating the competency of your staff and the team

2. Place workers with skills in jobs that will most benefit the project

3. Use incentives as a tool to motivate achievement of project goals or significant stepping-stones

4. Look at team building and keeping the team together

5. Establish staff development and training programs

6. Make use of mentors and mentoring to improve the skills and competency of staff members and the team

7. Consider the role of "chemistry" among team members and how it can affect the project in both positive and negative ways

8. Learn what you can do when the chemistry does not work

9. Recognize the effects of turnover on projects and find ways to deal with it.

Conventional wisdom tells us to determine *what* needs to be done first and then to select the appropriate person who has the knowledge and skills required to do it. However, in his book *Good to Great,* Jim Collins emphatically tells us: *first who . . . then what.* Rather than setting a direction, a vision, and a strategy for your project and then getting people committed and aligned, Collins and his research team found that great companies did just the opposite: They first selected the people who had the "right stuff" and then collaboratively set their course.

> ### *GOOD TO GREAT*
> ### JIM COLLINS
> ### Chapter 3: First Who . . . Then What[9]
>
> The executives who ignited the transformations from good to great did not first figure out where to drive the bus and then get people to take it there. No, they first got the right people on the bus (and the wrong people off the bus) and then figured out where to drive it. Their philosophy was: If we get the right people on the bus, the right people in the right seats, and the wrong people off the bus then we'll figure out how to take it someplace great. *Who* questions come before *what* decisions—before vision, before strategy, before rigorous discipline, consistently applied. The good-to-great leaders were rigorous, not ruthless, in people decisions. This means, when in doubt about a person, don't hire; when you know you need to make a people change, act; and put your best people on your biggest opportunities.

Establish a Great Team Structure

In Part II we talked about the concept of the core project leadership team. For large, complex projects, we recommend structuring the effort like a program consisting of multiple projects of varying levels of complexity. When structuring your program, establish a core *program* leadership team and multiple core *project* leadership teams that are small (four to six people, preferably only four), dedicated full-time to the project, co-located (preferably in a workroom), highly trained, and multi-skilled (typically a full-time project manager, business analyst, lead IT architect/developer, and business visionary). These core teams will augment their efforts by bringing in subject matter experts and forming subteams as needed.

Jim Highsmith, Director, Agile Project Management Practice, and Fellow, Business Technology Council at Cutter Consortium, identifies the components of large, adaptive project teams:[10]

> ➤ *Hub organizational structure.* Like the core team structure introduced in Chapter 4, the hub organizational structure reflects aspects of both hierarchical and network structures. This model may comprise several customer teams, numerous feature teams, an architecture team, a verification and validation team, and a project management team. Teams take on all possible configurations: virtual, co-located, or a combination.

> ➤ *Self-organization extensions.* As the number of teams within the project expands, the organizational structure transitions from a team framework to a project framework within which multiple teams operate. Creating a self-organizing team framework involves (1) getting the right leaders, (2) communicating the work breakdown and integration strategies, (3) encouraging interaction and information flow between teams, and (4) framing project-wide decision-making. Obviously, as more teams are formed, complexity increases. Managing inter-team dependencies is critical; teams need to fully understand their boundaries and their interdependencies.

> ➤ *Team self-discipline.* Behaviors required of teams when working in this structure include: (1) accept accountability for team results, (2) engage

collaboratively with other teams, (3) work within the project organization framework, and (4) balance project goals with team goals.

The composition of great teams is important. Research has shown that successful teams have a ". . . diverse membership—not of race and gender, but of old blood and new. New team members clearly added creative spark and critical links to the experience of the entire industry. Unsuccessful teams were isolated from each other, whereas the members of successful teams were interconnected . . . across a giant cluster of artists and scientists. Pay special attention to team composition, striking a balance between diversity and cohesion. Diversity is needed for new collaborations, while cohesion comes from repeat collaborations."[11]

Empower Your Team Members

The complex project manager delegates by deciding which roles and responsibilities to keep and which to entrust to others. The goal is to achieve shared, distributed leadership. In addition, the project manager determines which procedures to standardize across sub-teams and which to allow others to tailor. For example, the overall program may follow one cycle while allowing sub-teams to follow other cycles. The program may use a variant of the waterfall model, with highly structured phases and decision gates, but allow individual projects to use agile techniques to achieve their individual objectives.

Build a Culture of Discipline

Taking advice once again from Jim Collins, it is important to build a culture of discipline.[12] It is a commonly held misconception that the imposition of standards and discipline discourages creativity. A project team is like a start-up company. To truly innovate, the team needs to value creativity, imagination, and risk-taking. However, to maintain a sense of control over a large team, we often impose structure, insist on planning, and institutionalize coordination systems of meetings and reports.

The risk of requiring too much rigor is that the team becomes bureaucratic. Collins calls this the "entrepreneurial death spiral." He contends that ". . . bureaucracy is imposed to compensate for incompetence and lack of discipline—a problem that largely goes away if you have the right people in the first place." The goal is to learn how to use rigor and discipline to *enable* creativity.

GOOD TO GREAT
JIM COLLINS
A Culture of Discipline[13]

All companies have a culture, some companies have discipline, but few companies have a culture of discipline.

- Sustained great results depend upon building a culture full of self-disciplined people who take disciplined action.
- A culture of discipline involves duality. On the one hand, it involves people who adhere to a consistent system; on the other hand, it gives people freedom and responsibility.
- A culture of discipline is about having disciplined people who engage in disciplined thought and who then take disciplined action.
- When you have disciplined thought, you don't need bureaucracy. When you have disciplined action, you don't need excessive controls. When you combine a culture of discipline with an ethic of entrepreneurship, you get the magical alchemy of great performance.

Lead, Don't Manage, Contractor Teams

Traditional fixed-price contracts assume requirements stability and are prescriptive in nature, which is appropriate for well-understood, predictable projects. However, when the project must adapt as more is learned and business needs change, typical contracts are less appropriate. For complex, adaptive projects, the goal is to move away from long, detailed contracts toward relationship-based partnerships. Seek out contractors that focus on people, innovation, and research and development. Consider establishing a co-located design center where contractor and internal teams work collaboratively to help define and develop the problem and solution. Establish contracts that fix time and budget but allow scope to fluctuate under a predetermined, controlled process.

Nonetheless, some contract terms may be helpful. Consider adding terms for managing the contractor team that encourage collaboration and flexibility (e.g., joint planning sessions, integrated project schedules, earned value management, control-gate reviews, award fees, penalties). Document and communicate expectations and establish clear evaluation criteria. Develop and use a team operating agreement. Conduct regular progress evaluations and periodic reviews of contract terms and conditions.

Use Virtual Teams as a Strategic Advantage

Virtual teams whose members are geographically dispersed, multicultural, and cross-functional, yet work on highly interdependent tasks, present unique leadership challenges. Leaders of all teams, whether dispersed or co-located, have responsibilities they must fulfill, including communicating the vision, establishing expectations and an achievable strategy to reach the vision, and creating a positive team environment. It can be difficult to carry out these responsibilities at a distance. Arvind Malhotra, Ann Majchrzak, and Benson Rosen conducted research and identified six practices of effective leaders of virtual teams:[14]

1. Establish and maintain trust through the use of communication technology

2. Ensure that distributed diversity is understood and appreciated

3. Manage virtual work-life cycles (meetings)

4. Monitor team progress using technology

5. Enhance the visibility of virtual members within the team and outside in the organization

6. Enable individual members of the virtual team to benefit from the team.

For complex projects involving virtual team members, communication and collaboration are the lifeblood of the team. Communication manners, methods, and frequencies are crucial factors in determining the success or failure of virtual teams, so develop a communication strategy early in the project. Remember that there is no substitute for face-to-face sessions when the team is in early formative stages or in crisis. Make the effort to travel to the virtual team location to collaborate and build strong relationships that can then be sustained virtually. If your sponsor indicates that travel is too expensive, explain that you can't afford *not* to establish a trusting relationship—and it can only be done in person.

In today's electronically borderless world, technology is an enabler for us to keep in close touch, manage interdependencies, and resolve issues. Audio conferencing, web meetings, and email are the rule of the day for progress reporting and quick decision-making. Paper-based communication takes on enormous importance when virtual teams are involved. Learn the art of keeping adequate documentation without overburdening the team. Formal procedures and processes are necessary to set and maintain expectations.

According to Michelle LaBrosse, founder of Cheetah Learning, the challenge is not finding the right tools: ". . . the biggest barriers are often around communications and work culture. Ground rules that focus on them can increase your team's productivity and let you reap the rewards of the virtual workforce." LaBrosse goes on to list several best practices for working with virtual teams:[15]

> *Build trust.* Trust is built when you bring your team together for training or team-building, and then continues to grow when leaders set and the team meets clear expectations consistently.

> *Manage results, not activity.* In the virtual environment, when you can't see what people are doing, the key is to manage results. Set expectations and monitor results, not daily activities.

> *Schedule regular communication.* It is important to establish a regular time for reporting progress and managing issues.

> *Create communication that saves time, not that kills it.* With the empowerment created by email comes the weight of managing it. Having to respond to hundreds of emails every day can become a barrier to effectiveness. Clearly, email is a critical tool in our work environments. The project leader's job is to ensure that the team's email communication is as efficient and productive as possible.

> *Create standards that build a culture of discipline.* With a virtual team, you need to focus on creating a sense of cohesion and pride in being part of the team and the larger enterprise. Make sure your teams know

your quality standards and expectations to avoid rework, disappointments, and ultimately, delays.

➤ *Define rules of responsiveness.* Whether your team is working remotely or is co-located, it is necessary to define rules of responsiveness. How quickly are people expected to return an email or a phone call? What is your protocol when people are out of the office or on vacation? If you're in a customer service environment, it's important to have clear expectations regarding how to respond to all customer inquiries.

By implementing these commonsense practices, virtual teams can be more productive than traditional teams. Manage your virtual teams well and they will become a strategic advantage.

Encourage Innovation through Edge-of-Chaos Leadership

Large project teams are complex adaptive systems, and as such, they are constantly self-organizing, evolving, and adapting to changes in their environment within and outside the project. The role of the complex project manager is more about team leadership than project management. Using complexity thinking, the project manager does not intervene when project teams are adapting to changes and appear to be in chaos. As we have seen, our traditional approaches—predicting, goal-setting, planning, monitoring, and controlling—may inhibit the team from organizing itself into a dynamic, creative group that then determines (or better yet, *lets emerge*) the optimal team organization and the most innovative solution. The wise project manager gets out of the way of a dynamic, self-organizing team of experts by encouraging experimentation and questioning, providing inspiration, and striving to create an environment where each member can be authentic and can arrive at decisions without any predetermined biases.

Using complexity thinking, the project manager tolerates opposite views by balancing them to such a degree that they become complementary rather than cancel each other out. In addition, heuristic rules will emerge as the group gels and becomes a cohesive team. The project manager strives to unite team members in a common goal to be different, unique, and creative, constantly examining contradictions and inconsistencies. No options or alternatives are excluded from consideration, no one optimal solution is believed to exist, and uncertainty in decision-making is widely tolerated.[16]

Warren Bennis notes that leaders of great groups encourage dissent and diversity in pursuit of the shared vision, understanding the difference between healthy dissent and self-serving obstructionism—a critical trait in leading edge-of-chaos teams. Leaders of great groups can discern what people in the group need. Bennis identifies four behavioral traits of these leaders:[17]

➤ Provide direction and meaning

➤ Generate and sustain trust

➤ Display a bias toward action, risk-taking, and curiosity

➤ Are purveyors of hope.

Edge-of-chaos management will likely make traditional project managers quite uncomfortable at first. But as you experiment with it, use it, and witness the power of teams when they are encouraged to adapt and evolve, you will become passionate about honing your ability to become a situational project leader of complex teams, adapting your style to the needs of the team.

Manage Agile Teams with a Light Touch

As the iterative and agile methodologies mature, project managers need to develop new approaches to team leadership. Sanjiv Augustine offers several principles and practices for managing teams that are using iterative, incremental development and adaptable methods:[18]

➤ Foster alignment and cooperation

➤ Encourage emergence and self-organization

➤ Institute learning and adaptation.

Agile project management practices include:

➤ *Organic teams.* Enable connections and adaptation through close relationships on small, flexible teams.

➤ *Guiding vision.* Keep the team aligned and directed with a shared mental model.

➤ *Simple rules.* Establish a set of simple, generative process rules for the team.

➤ *Open information.* Provide free and open access to information.

➤ *Light touch.* Apply intelligent control to foster emergent order and maximal value.

➤ *Adaptive leadership.* Steer the project by continuously monitoring, learning, and adapting.

CASE STUDY: LARGE, DISPERSED, DIVERSE TEAMS
Transforming a Global Development Team[19]

Consider the dilemma of a U.S.-based financial services organization operating in more than 50 countries with 90,000 employees. The leadership team was convinced that they were not harnessing the power of their development teams, which were located all around the globe. The teams were operating in silos; there was very little collaboration and sharing of best practices. A huge organization, the company recognized that it needed to leverage the knowledge and expertise of individuals across the company, ensuring more focus on the design and creation of integrated and reusable components to increase innovation and reduce redundant development and inefficiencies.

The organization enlisted the help of a consulting firm to develop a program designed to promote development and management best practices based on real-world scenarios. The strategy to leverage the power of the global development team was to create a change program to introduce best practices to the senior engineers while increasing their technical and management skills. The program shared technical best practices using real-life case studies.

The company achieved its key objective: increasing communication and collaboration among members of a global team of engineers. In addition, the participants refined their problem-solving skills and their ability to build innovative solutions efficiently. The company also realized the benefits of creating a cohesive organization across its engineering population, enhanced career opportunities for the participants, and confirmed its commitment to top technical talent.

TEAM COLLABORATION, COMMUNICATION, AND COORDINATION

"Collaborative management techniques bridge the needs of developers, project managers, and infrastructure operations staff to ensure the applications needed to support e-business can be built quickly and managed effectively."

—CHAOS REPORT, THE STANDISH GROUP

For effective team collaboration, communication, and coordination, we recommend the following practices:

➤ Use a standard formal methodology

➤ Insist on collaborative planning

➤ Acquire state-of-the-art collaboration tools.

Use a Standard Formal Methodology

The Standish Group found that 46 percent of successful projects used a formal project management methodology. For complex projects, using a standard methodology—while encouraging each team to tailor it as needed—goes a long way toward eliminating unknown cross-team dependencies.

RECIPE FOR PROJECT SUCCESS: THE CHAOS TEN
The Standish Group International, Inc. 2001
#8: Formal Methodology:[20]

When using a formal methodology, certain steps and procedures are reproducible and reusable; thus, the tendency to reinvent the wheel is minimized and project-wide consistency is maximized. Lessons learned from previous projects can be incorporated into your project approach. The process encourages a go or no-go decision checkpoint. A project team can proceed with a higher level of confidence or steps can be either halted or altered to fit changing requirements. The ability to adjust in real time enhances project skills and reduces project risk.

When developing a formal methodology:

1. Include a problem statement in your formal methodology to ensure that everyone is solving the same business problem.
2. Establish a formal process for gathering and maintaining requirements.
3. Develop a detailed plan.
4. Understand that one missed small detail can cause big problems that could lead to project failure (the "butterfly effect").
5. Consider using analogies to improve communication between users and developers.
6. Maintain a formal methodology to support interactions between stakeholders.
7. Consider establishing a project management office.
8. Integrate formal peer reviews into your formal process.
9. Employ a flexible, formal process to improve the success rate.

Lessons learned about tools supporting the methodology include:[21]

1. Use a standard vocabulary to facilitate proper communications.
2. Use requirements management tools; these can have a huge impact on the success of a project.
3. Consider using change management software, which has many benefits in the dynamic world of developing application software.
4. Consider using a collaboration tool like WebEx, which can be especially useful for distributed and geographically dispersed teams.

5. Use inspection and testing tools like you would use spell check on documents—application software bugs are the leading cause of downtime.
6. Consider the benefits of a standard infrastructure.
7. Learn how to recognize trustworthy and untrustworthy vendors.
8. Consider the benefits of using open source software and components to jump-start a project and provide the baseline.
9. Use cost, risk, and gain as the central factors to optimizing your project portfolio and requirements set.

Do not overly burden the various teams with standards, but do insist on those that are needed to provide a realistic view of the overall project and to manage cross-team dependencies. Enforce the use of standard collaboration procedures, practices, and tools. Be firm about establishing decision checkpoints that involve all core project team members at critical junctures.

Insist on Collaborative Planning

Involve all core team members in the project planning process and seek feedback often to continually improve the performance of the team. Use face-to-face working sessions during planning meetings, especially for scoping, scheduling, identifying risks and dependencies, and conducting critical control-gate reviews. When preparing your project budget, be sure to include adequate time and budget to bring core team members together for these critical sessions.

Acquire State-of-the-Art Collaboration Tools

Secure best-in-class software tools to enable collaboration and document-sharing. Two general types of collaboration tools are available: professional service automation (PSA), which is designed to optimize service engagements; and enterprise project management (EPM) tool suites, which are used to manage multiple projects. In addition, provide your team members with personal communication and telecommunications tools so that they feel closely tied and connected. If these tools are an unconventional expense item for projects in your organizational culture, educate your project sponsor on the criticality of collaboration, stressing the need to manage the cross-project interdependencies that are known at the start of the project as well as those that will emerge along the way.

SOCIAL SOFTWARE[22]

"Social software" is web-enabled programs that allow users to interact and share data with other users. This computer-mediated communication has become very popular with sites like MySpace and YouTube and has resulted in large user bases and billion-dollar purchases of the software and their communities by large corporations (News Corp purchased MySpace and Google purchased YouTube). The more specific term "collaborative software" applies to cooperative information-sharing systems and is usually narrowly applied to the software that enables collaborative work functions.

Social software allows groups of people to interact and share information like never before. For example, groups are able to chat directly with tech support when trying to resolve an issue with a product or a process. Web-based video conferencing and collaboration is another example of social software.

There is no stopping a great team. However, great teams do not happen by accident. Hard work, planning, and disciplined effort are required to convert a group of people into a high-performing team. For complex projects the effort is magnified because multiple large, geographically dispersed, and culturally diverse teams are involved. Leaders of complex projects cease to be project managers and become leaders of teams.

What are the elements of superior team leadership? We have discovered that it takes an understanding of the complexities of large, diverse teams as well as a keen realization of the power, wisdom, and *potential* of teams. To be a great team leader, you must focus on these areas:

- Make sure you are appropriately experienced and seasoned to be at the helm of a complex initiative; then, insist that the other key project roles are filled with senior project leaders.
- Learn how to build a great team; devote a significant amount of your time to ensuring that your teams are healthy, well-structured, and consist of the right people.
- Nurture your teams, but also get out of the way and empower them to perform their magic.
- Pay special attention to contractor teams; lead them with the same degree of professionalism as your internal teams.
- Use virtual teams as a strategic advantage, but make sure you have adequate face time with them.
- Encourage experimentation, questioning, and innovation through edge-of-chaos leadership; the results will astound you.
- Lead the teams with a strong focus on collaboration, communications, and coordination.

As you begin to build your teams, remember that you will need a combination of adaptive and conventional project management techniques in your toolbox (see Table 10-2).

Managing Large, Dispersed, Culturally Diverse Project Teams	
Complexities	**Management Approaches**

• Many complex adaptive teams
• Human behaviors impossible to predict
• Multi-layered, interdependent teams
  – Geographically dispersed
  – Culturally diverse
  – Virtual
  – Multi-skilled
• Dissimilar procedures, practices, and tools leading to integration issues
• Risk management inadequacies and inconsistencies, leading to unknown events
• Integration of interdependent components produced by different teams
	Adaptive
	• Establish an experienced leadership team.
	• Leverage the power of teams
	• Build great teams
	• Use edge-of-chaos management when appropriate
	• Empower agile teams instilled with a culture of discipline
	• Use virtual teams as a strategic asset
	• Insist on face-to-face meetings for key planning and decision-making
	
	Conventional
	• Manage contractor teams
	• Insist on standard procedures and tools when appropriate
	• Establish a culture of collaboration and open communication

TABLE 10-2. Approaches for Managing Large, Dispersed, Culturally Diverse Project Teams

NOTES

1. Christian Jensen, Staffan Johansson, and Mikael Lofstrom, "Project Relationships–A Model for Analyzing Interactional Uncertainty," *International Journal of Project Management* (2006), vol. 24, no. 1.

2. Jon R. Katzenbach and Douglas K. Smith, *The Wisdom of Teams* (Boston: Harvard Business School Press, 1993), 20–21.

3. Warren Bennis, "The Secrets of Great Groups," Leader to Leader Institute (1997). Online at http://pfdf.org/leaderbooks/121/winter97/bennis.html (accessed October 2007).

4. Jon R. Katzenbach and Douglas K. Smith, *The Wisdom of Teams* (Boston: Harvard Business School Press, 1993), 2–6.

5. Ibid., 24–26.

6. Jim Johnson, *My Life is Failure: 100 Things You Should Know to be a Successful Project Leader* (West Yarmouth, MA: The Standish Group International, 2006), 10.

7. Aaron Shenhar et al., "Toward a NASA-Specific Project Management Framework," *Engineering Management Journal* (2005), vol. 17, no. 4.

8. Jim Johnson, *My Life is Failure: 100 Things You Should Know to be a Successful Project Leader* (West Yarmouth, MA: The Standish Group International, 2006), 12.

9. Jim Collins, *Good to Great* (New York: HarperCollins Publishers, Inc., 2001), 50–64.

10. Jim Highsmith, *Agile Project Management: Creating Innovative Products* (Boston: Addison-Wesley, 2004), 235–251.

11. Peggy King, "Dream Teams Thrive on Mix of Old and New Blood," Kellogg School of Management News and Information (2002). Online at http://www.kellogg.northwestern.edu/news/whatsnew/Uzziresearch2005.htm (accessed February 2008).

12. Jim Collins, *Good to Great* (New York: HarperCollins Publishers, Inc., 2001), 120–143.

13. Ibid.

14. Arvind Malhotra, Ann Majchrzak, and Benson Rosen, "Leading Virtual Teams," Academy of Management (2007), vol. 21, no. 1. Online at http://aom.metapress.com/app/home/contribution.asp?referrer=parent&backto=issue,5,10;journal,4,8;linkingpublicationresults,1:120012,1 (accessed February 2008).

15. Michelle LaBrosse, "Virtual Velocity: Effective Project Management Gives Virtual Teams the Edge." Online at http://www.projecttimes.com/index.php?option=com_content&task=view&id=141&Itemid=30 (accessed March 2008).

16. Vladimir Dimitrov, "Thinking and Working in Complexity." Online at http://www.zulrmry.com/VladimirDimitrov/pages/think.html (accessed January 2008).

17. Warren Bennis, "The Secrets of Great Groups," Leader to Leader Institute (1997). Online at http://pfdf.org/leaderbooks/121/winter97/bennis.html (accessed October 2007).

18. Sanjiv Augustine, *Managing Agile Projects* (Upper Saddle River, NJ: Prentice Hall Professional Technical Reference, 2005), 25, 43–186.

19. Thoughtworks, "Transforming a Global Development Team: A Case Study." Online at http://www.thoughtworks.com/our-clients/case-studies/global-team-transformation.html (accessed March 2008).

20. Jim Johnson, *My Life is Failure: 100 Things You Should Know to be a Successful Project Leader* (West Yarmouth, MA: The Standish Group International, 2006), 13.

21. Ibid., 15.

22. http://www.gantthead.com/content/articles/240180.cfm

CHAPTER 11
Applying Complexity Thinking to Highly Innovative, Urgent Projects

Complexity Dimensions	Project Profile		
	Independent	Moderately Complex	Highly Complex
Urgency and Flexibility of Cost, Time, and Scope	• Minimized scope • Small milestones • Flexible schedule, budget, and scope	• Schedule, budget, scope can undergo minor variations, but deadlines are firm • Achievable scope and milestones	• Over-ambitious schedule and scope • Deadline is aggressive, fixed, and cannot be changed • Budget, scope, and quality have no room for flexibility

An urgent project that demands an innovative solution and has an aggressive scope and schedule is another type of complex project. In this chapter we recommend management techniques that can help you and your team manage the complexities involved while establishing and maintaining an environment of adaptability, innovation, and creativity.

WHAT MAKES HIGHLY INNOVATIVE, URGENT PROJECTS COMPLEX?

Urgent projects, by their very nature, are different from what we consider to be traditional projects. Traditional projects are usually started with a defined scope, budget, and timeline, and an attempt is made to follow a prescribed methodology. Urgent projects are seldom started this way. For urgent projects, time is critical for project success; delays mean a high probability of project failure. Crisis situations such as war and natural disasters are examples of urgent projects.

NONTRADITIONAL PROJECT START-UP METHODS

Urgent projects come in two varieties: those that are planned and deemed to be top priority and those that are unexpected—i.e., they were not planned or budgeted but suddenly arise because of an unforeseen critical event. Whether planned or unexpected, urgent projects usually have several things in common: Cost is not an issue, time is of the essence, and they receive top priority for resources across the organization.

HIGH STAKES

Examples of urgent projects abound in the intelligence community. Whether developing an innovative new device for the agents in the field or a faster, better way to collect and analyze intelligence information, the stakes are high. Cost and process are of no concern, but time and accuracy are critical.

High-stakes projects involve numerous complexities:

➤ There is little time to experiment, create, innovate, or ensure that we have the "best" solution—the team must act quickly to resolve the burning need.

➤ The team strives to produce an environment for the project that is free from demands or dependencies on any other groups, projects, or business units; thus, the inevitable interrelationships and dependencies are often not discovered until the new product is in the field.

➤ Multiple urgent project teams operating concurrently run the risk of duplicating efforts, or even worse, fielding solutions that are disharmonious instead of complementary, possibly leading to confusion, mistakes, and misinformation.

HOW TO LEAD HIGHLY INNOVATIVE, URGENT PROJECTS

Fixed deadlines almost always add risk to projects because the time factor is interdependent with other competing demands, including project scope, quality, risk, and cost. Economists have been warning us for years that success in the 21st century is contingent on our ability to produce innovative products swiftly to meet growing demands in emerging markets. The fiercely competitive marketplace has imposed a grinding sense of urgency on almost all innovation projects.

For urgent projects to succeed, they need a project team that operates like a special task force, staffed with handpicked members who are focused solely on resolving the crisis swiftly. Procedures are simplified, if not abandoned completely, and senior management is highly involved and supportive.[1] Our recommendations center on the differences between leading planned urgent projects, which usually involve innovation, and managing unplanned urgent projects, which are usually driven by unexpected events.

PLANNED URGENT PROJECTS

To make planned urgent projects successful, we are able to take the time to set up the appropriate infrastructure. Critical steps include:

➤ Establish permanent, flexible innovation teams

➤ Assign the best resources

➤ Time-box the effort.

CASE STUDY: PLANNED URGENT INNOVATION PROJECTS
**Toshiba: Transitioning to an Agile
Company by Creating a Boundary-Spanning
Innovation Division**

Toshiba uses special units that transcend typical organizational boundaries and are usually focused on innovation, emerging markets, and new business ventures with great potential. These special operations teams are flexibly structured and highly connected via the Internet and periodic face-to-face meetings. The goals of Toshiba's special innovation teams are to:[2]

• Intensify the sense of speed and agility

• Change the fiscal-period mindset

• Create a boundaryless operation/partnership

• Invest to get an early foothold in emerging markets.

Examples of highly successful new products that Toshiba propelled into the marketplace through the use of these teams include the DVD, wireless communication infrastructure, and digital broadcasting.

Establish Flexible, Permanent Innovation Teams

Although planned urgent projects can originate from any business unit, they are often managed through special units that transcend typical organizational boundaries and are focused on innovation, emerging markets, and new business ventures. These special operations teams are flexibly structured and highly connected via the Internet and periodic face-to-face meetings. To succeed these groups need executive support from the highest levels of the organization—and full funding. Some organizations establish the innovation teams as a separate new product development division, while others establish one "urgent project team" that spans all divisions and works on projects that meet predefined criteria.

Assign the Best Resources

Team members on urgent projects must have the skills, information, and motivation to make decisions with little data and to adapt to change quickly. They must also be able to move freely from project to project as priorities change. Flexible and agile project management, business analysis, and systems engineering procedures and tools, along with a project sponsor who is available in real time, all combine to provide the foundation for this flexibility.

Time-box the Effort

While we all hate fixed deadlines, a time-boxed schedule increases the level of urgency the project team feels and forces decisions to be made quickly and efficiently. Most innovation teams are given a fixed time within which to design and deliver new products. A few years ago, most urgent projects were expected to be completed within 18 months. Now it seems that urgent project teams are under constant pressure to deliver even faster.

Structure the time-boxed schedule into a series of iterations, each marked by the completion of a major deliverable. Conduct reviews after each iteration to ensure the quality of the deliverables and to move quickly into the next iteration. This approach frees the team to focus on the work needed to complete the current iteration only. To meet time pressures, eliminate all "nice-to-haves" and unnecessary features. Initially, deliver the *minimum workable solution* to test the viability of the concept in the marketplace.

UNEXPECTED URGENT PROJECTS

For unexpected urgent projects, the initial environment is truly one of chaos. A sense of urgency imbues everyone—project team members and stakeholders alike—with a clear focus and a strong motivation to perform. Consider the rescuers after a major disaster. Firefighters and paramedics are highly trained and skilled; nevertheless, events (such as Hurricane Katrina and the 9/11 attack) occur for which we are woefully unprepared. The essential elements of success when an unexpected urgent situation arises include establishing and maintaining a sense of urgency and implementing proven critical practices.

Establish and Maintain a Sense of Urgency by Adapting to the Situation

What happens in unplanned, urgent circumstances? Often, routine procedures are abandoned and teams form around anyone who shows leadership. Teams form and re-form according to the need, sometimes following protocol, sometimes making it up as they go along—*adapting to their environment.* It is no secret that really urgent projects can be carried out in record time using unconventional, sometimes radical techniques.

Management techniques we recommend for urgent, unstable situations with a high degree of uncertainty include:

➤ Staff the project with flexible, high-performing team members who welcome unorthodox practices

➤ Make it clear to team members and stakeholders that time drives all decisions

➤ Become involved at the management level only in dire situations.

Implement Proven Critical Practices

In a recent article in *Project Management Journal*®, entitled "Managing Unexpected Urgent Projects," Stephen Wearne, PhD, of the University of Manchester, UK, presented his findings from a study of six unexpected, urgent projects. The projects were diverse, across the globe, urgent, and highly successful. The projects Dr. Wearne studied were (1) launching the UK nationwide digital television transmission system in six months; (2) constructing an emergency river excess flood diversion system in two weeks; (3) installing a temporary deck structure spanning ruptured portions of a major highway bridge in seven weeks; (4) constructing a temporary power line 9.8 km long and connecting work to restore the power supply in 17 days; (5) restoring the tracks, power, and signaling systems over a main rail line in two weeks; and (6) sustaining seven months of work to sift, make safe, and remove 1.6 million tons of rubble, hazardous structural elements, and other wreckage to search for survivors, identify remains, and clear the 9/11 site.[3]

These projects demonstrate some of the practices that have proven to be successful in managing unexpected, urgent project. Indeed, the leadership team should consider these success factors for any complex project:

➤ *Assign full-time, temporary teams.* Teams from the study included contractors and consultants who were welcomed for their contribution to decision-making and problem-solving.

➤ *Use twinned leadership.* Relationships with stakeholders, outside authorities, and the news media were handled by a sponsor executive while the project manager focused on project execution.

➤ *Insist on face-to-face decision-making.* Traditional, hierarchical procedures were replaced with regular meetings attended by top managers who had the authority to make cost-related decisions and oral commitments.

➤ *Deploy all available resources.* Approved plans and budgets were developed during the work as needs arose. Suppliers and contractors were employed as partners, which allowed everyone to focus on meeting needs rather than protecting against risks. Cost-based rather than price-based terms of payment were used in all contracts.

➤ *Employ a proactive communication strategy.* The teams anticipated challenges involving stakeholders and the media, and they proactively established steering committees to agree on priorities, tasks, and roles and responsibilities.

➤ *Support teambuilding.* Managers and stakeholders recognized the value and necessity of building team relationships while the work was underway since there was no time to address this issue in advance.

➤ *Monitor changing perceptions of urgency.* Cost was not considered a factor in upfront decision-making based on the urgency of the projects.

However, as other priorities arose, project managers found that perceptions of urgency lessened over time. To avoid subsequent criticism for inappropriate expenditures, project managers should be alert to changing perceptions and manage expectations accordingly.

When leading planned urgent efforts, you will have the luxury of establishing the infrastructure that is needed for innovation to occur and to shorten the time-to-market as much as possible. It is critical to assign the most experienced, seasoned, passionate resources to urgent projects. This might mean that the most talented people are out of their divisions and working on an urgent project for up to 18 months. To avoid this situation, the best organizations establish permanent, flexible innovation teams that are separate from the operating divisions of the company and report directly to the CEO. Whichever structure is used, the urgent projects need to be time-boxed, funding cannot pose a barrier, and the team needs to implement the minimum viable solution.

For unplanned urgent projects, it is critical to establish and maintain a sense of urgency. If the sense of urgency is not established from the beginning, a debacle can result, as in the aftermath of Hurricane Katrina. If the pressure is relieved and the sense of urgency dissipates, time and attention will wane and the result will be disappointing at best. Even though you will be caught by surprise by the urgent need, stop long enough to implement critical factors that have proven to be successful in unexpected urgent situations. Once again, combine both conventional and adaptive approaches for managing planned or unplanned urgent projects (Table 11-1).

Managing Innovative, Urgent Projects	
Complexities	**Management Approaches**

•Urgent projects:
 – Planned – innovative products
 – Unplanned – unknown critical
   situations or events
•High stakes; highly visible
•Time rules, supersedes best practices
•Cost typically not an issue (but can
  becomes an issue if urgency wanes)
•Team struggles to remain independent
  of external constraints
•Process is thrown out
•Interdependencies are missed due to
  speed and isolation
•Sense of urgency fades
•Environment of confusion, mistakes, and
  misinformation
	Adaptive
	•Establish permanent, flexible innovation teams
	  or task forces
	•Handpick the best team members
	•Use "twinned leadership"
	•Time-box the effort; promote urgency
	•Deliver the minimum workable solution
	•Establish partnerships versus contractor
	  relationships
	•Insist on face-to-face decision-making
	•Deploy all available resources
	•Employ a proactive communication strategy to
	  maintain the sense of urgency
	•Support teambuilding
	•Monitor changing perceptions of urgency
	Conventional
	•Establish a time-boxed schedule
	 – Creates sense of urgency
	 – Forces decision-making
	•Conduct decision gate reviews

TABLE 11-1. Approaches for Managing Planned and Unplanned Urgent Projects

NOTES

1. Peter W. G. Morris and Jeffrey K. Pinto, *The Wiley Guide to Managing Projects* (Hoboken, NJ: John Wiley & Sons, Inc., 2004), 1280–1281.

2. Ikujiro Nonaka, *Knowledge Management: Critical Perspectives on Business and Management* (London: Taylor and Francis, 2005).

3. Stephen Wearne, "Managing Unexpected Urgent Projects," *Project Management Journal*® (December 2006). Online at http://www.allbusiness.com/management/4110865-1.html (accessed February 2008).

CHAPTER 12

Applying Complexity Thinking to Ambiguous Business Problems, Opportunities, and Solutions

Complexity Dimensions	Project Profile		
	Independent	**Moderately Complex**	**Highly Complex**
Clarity of Problem, Opportunity, and Solution	• Clear business objectives • Easily understood problem, opportunity, or solution	• Defined business objectives • Problem or opportunity is partially defined • Solution is partially defined	• Unclear business objectives • Problem or opportunity is ambiguous and undefined • Solution is difficult to define

"Successful problem solving requires finding the right solution to the right problem. We fail more often because we solve the wrong problem than because we get the wrong solution to the right problem."

—RUSSELL ACKOFF, SYSTEMS SCIENTIST

Complexity arises when managing a project with unclear business objectives and an ambiguous business problem or solution. Solutions that involve a widespread collection of systems functioning together also raise complexity issues. We offer techniques to help manage the complexities brought about by ambiguity, which requires an environment of adaptability, innovation, and creativity.

WHAT MAKES AMBIGUOUS PROJECTS COMPLEX?

Projects that involve an unclear business problem, an ambiguous business opportunity, or an undefined solution are essentially in a discovery or research and development mode. The problem or solution has not yet come into view with enough clarity to launch an implementation project.

AMBIGUOUS BUSINESS PROBLEM OR OPPORTUNITY

Complex projects often involve considerable uncertainty and ambiguity. When the business problem or opportunity is unclear, it is difficult to identify stakeholders, define business benefits, determine interdependencies, and establish project boundaries. Indeed, some would say that you cannot undertake a project if you cannot identify its business objectives.

AMBIGUOUS BUSINESS SOLUTION

Likewise, when the solution is ambiguous, it is impossible to assess the feasibility of the concept or to estimate costs. In this situation, we don't know where the solution lies on a continuum between proven, well-understood technology to groundbreaking innovation. As a result, all options must remain on the table until the team members are certain that they understand both the business problem or opportunity and the recommended solution sufficiently to move into an implementation phase. Solution uncertainty usually means that the project is charting new territory and will likely use new, unproven technologies.

CASE STUDY: AMBIGUOUS BUSINESS PROBLEM
IT Legacy Replacement

Consider the situation that many large companies are facing today: Their existing legacy systems are old, outmoded, and fragile. In the case of one large financial institution, the core system for processing financial transactions (using 1960s batch-processing technology) could be run only on weekends. When problems occurred and the system crashed, the processing had to be started over from the beginning and the system would not be updated with current information at the start of the work week. Clearly, the legacy system needed to be replaced. Additionally, plans were underway to relocate the operations center halfway across the country.

The objective was clear: Develop a new IT operating system and hire, train, and set in motion a newly formed team at the same time. However, the business requirements were unclear, having been buried in the legacy system for many years. The business units were experiencing difficulties defining and reaching agreement on requirements for several reasons: (1) politically, there was a lack of consensus among management, (2) users were unable to define requirements because of a lack of knowledge of how the current processes and systems worked, and (3) there was no clear vision about how the business should operate in the future.

The solution: Create a small "skunk works" team led by a mid-level operations manager who understood how the current system worked (with all its flaws and workarounds) and had a vision of the organization's future business needs. This business visionary was paired with a lead technologist who had an IT team of nearly 100 professionals to design and develop the system. This team was empowered to make all decisions and was supported by senior management. The operations center opened with key people who had been transferred from their original locations, an entire new operations staff, and a brand new IT application system and data center. When the expected problems associated with implementing a major new IT application arose, they were resolved and the operations center was running smoothly within a few months.

HOW TO LEAD AMBIGUOUS PROJECTS

Ambiguity and uncertainty are the hallmarks of complex projects. We present recommendations for leading projects when the business problem or opportunity is ambiguous and when the nature of the business solution is ambiguous.

AMBIGUOUS BUSINESS PROBLEM OR OPPORTUNITY

In an uncertain project environment characterized by ambiguous business problems or opportunities, we suggest that the project leader:

➤ Focus initial efforts on determining a clear business objective

➤ Embrace professional business analysis.

Focus Initial Efforts on Determining a Clear Business Objective

Without clear business objectives, a project does not yet exist. Before commencing work, conduct interviews with the project sponsor and key stakeholders to determine their business objectives, expectations, and constraints. Any obvious inconsistencies in the expectations of key stakeholders must be resolved before actual project work begins. A good place to start is by securing approval to form a small expert team to study the business problem or opportunity and determine the best project approach.

RECIPE FOR PROJECT SUCCESS: THE CHAOS TEN
The Standish Group International, Inc. 2001
#4: Clear Business Objectives

Clear business objectives—a clear understanding of where the business is today and what the organization wants in the future to achieve strategic goals—is essential to project success. Business objectives may include customer satisfaction, increased revenue, or decreased cost.[1]

1. Be certain that everyone involved is on the same page in terms of the project's business objectives.

2. Make sure stakeholders can recite the "elevator pitch," a concise and comprehensible explanation of the business objectives delivered in 10 seconds or less.

3. Consider the big picture and how the project fits into the organization's overall strategy.

4. Promote speed and understand how clarity of business objectives can increase speed.

5. Have a yardstick for measuring progress on the project.

6. Make return on investment a clear business objective.

7. Collaborate with team members to ensure a clear and concise message on business objectives.

8. Build the foundation for a peer review process.

9. Avoid having too many cooks; too many stakeholders can spoil the project.

10. Do your homework through basic and fundamental research and test the clarity and reliability of the business objectives.

Embrace Professional Business Analysis

Professional business analysis is an emerging discipline (see www.theiiba .org). Organizations that acquire and master business analysis competencies and elevate business analysts to a leadership role will be equipped to react to and even preempt changes in the marketplace, flowing value through the enterprise to the customer and thereby achieving a competitive advantage.

The business analyst plays a significant role in helping the executive team translate business strategies into business initiatives. The business analyst guides an array of enterprise analysis activities leading up to project definition and funding. Organizations will use some or all of these techniques, depending on the maturity of their portfolio management and business analysis practices. It is important to note that while these activities seem to be performed in sequence, many occur concurrently and some may be omitted altogether.

The analysis techniques that are designed to bring the business problem, opportunity, and recommended solution into view include the following:[2]

➤ Creating and maintaining the business architecture to bring engineering principles to bear when managing organizational changes

➤ Conducting feasibility analyses to determine the optimal solution approach to a business opportunity or problem, delaying design decisions until the last responsible moment

➤ Developing a decision package of information for proposed new projects for the portfolio management team, including scoping and defining new business opportunities, preparing the business case, and conducting the initial risk assessment

➤ Preparing and presenting the new project proposal to the project sponsor for disposition

➤ Managing the projected business benefits throughout the project and measuring the business benefits of the deployed solution.

Embrace practices that use business models and visualization techniques that can help clarify the current and target states of the business. Spend ample time researching and studying the business problem or opportunity; conducting competitive, technological, and benchmark studies; defining dependencies and interrelationships; and identifying potential options for meeting the business need or solving the business problem.

AMBIGUOUS BUSINESS SOLUTION

We offer the following recommendations to enable the project leader and team to make progress despite an uncertain solution approach:

➤ Form a special "innovation team"

➤ Use edge-of-chaos management to bring the solution into view

➤ Become an expert at facilitating teams to make innovative decisions

➤ Conduct a feasibility study to identify and analyze solution options

➤ Conduct value-chain analysis for cross-functional enterprise solutions

➤ Conduct root-cause analysis to ensure the solution will solve the business problem

➤ Become adept at using tools and techniques that foster creativity and innovation

➤ Lead your team into "the zone."

CASE STUDY: AMBIGUOUS SOLUTION
Retail Business Intelligence Project

For an example of a project involving an ambiguous solution, we look to the retail industry. Many retailers store information on what their customers purchase and use loyalty cards to identify each customer. A major supermarket chain decided to use the shopping history held on a central database to identify special offers that would be of particular interest to a customer when he or she arrived at the checkout and presented a loyalty card.

In this case, the system held a record of all the items the customer had purchased during the last six months; the supermarket had approximately nine million customers every day, each purchasing an average of about 30 items. Although the project seemed attractive from a commercial viewpoint, it would have involved searching a four-terabyte centralized database, analyzing the results, and delivering the information remotely—almost instantaneously to all stores concurrently. Given the existing system architecture, this was impossible. While a change to the system architecture (e.g., distributing the database to stores or caching data locally) might have made the system viable, the cost of doing so would have far outweighed the business benefit.[3]

Clearly, both the business team and the IT team had leapt to the solution without conducting due diligence to fully understand the business problem and determine the most feasible and innovative solution.

Form a Special Innovation Team

As we learned in Chapter 11, innovation comes most readily when special teams are established, removed from the day-to-day operations of the business, fully funded, fully supported from the top, and time-boxed. When the solution is elusive and the project is critical, adopt practices learned from organizations that have successfully established special innovation teams—

and then get out of the way! Assign a project manager who has exceptional technical skills, has a highly flexible style, and is comfortable working with uncertainty.

Use Edge-of-Chaos Management to Bring the Solution into View

In some circumstances, when a project seems to be operating on the edge of chaos, the team is still brainstorming, creating, studying, examining ideas, and evaluating dependencies to select the most valuable, most elegant, and least complex solution. Encourage lots of experimentation and prototyping to bring the solution into focus early in the project. In rare cases, project teams design and develop more than one solution in order to determine which approach to pursue. Use small-scale prototypes to test concepts and new technologies. Adopt the practices of three to five design cycles and late design freeze. When this "tiger team" approach is used, the outcome can be more innovative and creative than ever imagined. If your team seems to be operating on the edge of chaos, it might be just the right place to be!

Become an Expert at Facilitating Teams to Make Innovative Decisions

Decision-making in the context of complex and ambiguous projects is wrought with pitfalls. Because we are attempting to clarify ambiguities, we are reluctant to make any decisions until the business situation is unambiguous and our solution approach is defined. However, decisions are necessary to make forward progress. We are also reluctant to make decisions until the results and ramifications of our decisions are well understood. However, in complex projects, that is virtually impossible.

Various approaches to decision-making are appropriate at different times throughout complex projects. Again, the *situational project leader* determines the appropriate decision-making approach depending on the situation. These decision-making approaches include:[4]

➤ Decisions are made independently, by the project manager or a small group, mostly through intuition. This approach is most appropriate early in the project when little information has been discovered but forward progress is critical.

➤ Decisions are made collaboratively, with a team of experts striving to arrive at the most innovative, creative decision. This approach is most appropriate for identifying potential solution approaches to the business need and for identifying new products for the marketplace. When creativity and innovation are the goal, this decision-making approach requires the project manager to foster edge-of-chaos behaviors to remove all current patterns and biases, striving for truly out-of-the-box thinking. The project manager must allow enough time to let ideas simmer and the solution emerge.

➤ Decisions are made using decision analysis techniques, i.e., based on the results of analysis as opposed to intuition, preference, or creativity. This highly scientific approach to decision-making involves the logical analysis of a correctly structured problem.

Decision analysis techniques are appropriate when it is important to remove all biases and prejudices from the decision. Decision analysis is applied during the enterprise analysis and architecture effort preceding project launch and subsequently as needed throughout the project. The decision analysis process typically involves four phases:

➤ Decision framing, or structuring the problem

➤ Modeling the alternatives

➤ Quantitative analysis

➤ Implementation, monitoring, and review of the decisions.

Conduct a Feasibility Study to Identify and Analyze Solution Options

Once a team of experts has participated in a creative brainstorming session to identify innovative solution options, the project manager should guide the team through an analysis of each option to determine which has the highest value and is most feasible.

The team analyzes the economic, technical, operational, cultural, safety, and legal feasibility of each solution option until it is clear which option(s) has a higher probability of success. The team then develops initial solution designs and prototypes to demonstrate its ability to manage solution dependencies and interrelationships. The team also conducts rigorous risk assessments and risk response planning for each option, focusing on identifying and managing interdependencies to external projects, groups, organizations, and application systems.

During the feasibility analysis, the team attempts to answer such questions as:

➤ Is this effort unprecedented? Have we, or anyone else, faced it before?

➤ Is the technology that is likely to be needed advanced (i.e., not commercially available) or even nonexistent?

➤ Do we understand the scientific phenomena involved (if any)?

➤ Is the problem within our business competence to solve? To understand?

➤ Is the problem/solution environment clear?

Conduct Value-Chain Analysis for Cross-Functional Enterprise Solutions

Value-chain analysis is an effective technique for assessing the feasibility of enterprise-wide solutions. Value-chain analysis attempts to describe the cross-functional processes within the organization and assesses the value that each activity within the process contributes to the organization's product or services. The goal is to ensure that the solution will be able to perform particular activities and to manage the interrelationships between the activities, resulting in a competitive advantage. The linkages can be flows of information, goods, and services as well as systems and processes.[5]

Conduct Root-Cause Analysis to Ensure the Solution Will Solve the Business Problem

Good solutions are designed to solve specific problems. Conduct thorough root-cause analysis to ensure that you have determined the underlying business problem. Cause mapping is a structured approach to problem-solving that is based on facts, data, and evidence. The goal is to remove biases and opinions from the process. Cause mapping creates a visual map that focuses on the entire system, i.e., any combination of the parts that function together as a whole. It can be used to solve all types of problems—errors, defects, failures, losses, outages, and incidents—in all types of industries.

Become Adept at Tools and Techniques That Foster Creativity and Innovation

An array of techniques is available to open minds to new ideas and to foster creativity and innovation. We present just a few for your consideration:[6]

> ➤ *Emotional intelligence.* Hone your emotional self to effectively use emotion in your communications, problem-solving, and decision-making.

Remember, people change behaviors because of their emotions—because they believe emotionally that doing so will be to their benefit.

➤ *Pattern discovery*. Use divergent thinking to discover new patterns that may lead to innovative ideas.

➤ *Metaphors and storytelling*. Use metaphors and imagery to add sensory and emotional richness to your understanding of a concept.

➤ *Mind mapping*. Create a visual representation of the components of an issue, with relationships and interdependencies depicted.

➤ *Visualization*. Use rich pictures, models, and simple diagrams to bring the project into view; visualization techniques ensure that all key stakeholders see the issue at hand the same way.

➤ *Intuition*. Trust your gut feelings, your instincts; intuition is one of the most powerful tools of the right brain, which can process vast amounts of information holistically and in record time.

➤ *Experimentation*. Intelligently choose experiments to conduct to remove uncertainty and ambiguity; as you learn, adapt appropriately.

➤ *Divergent thinking*. Explore options, connections, and relationships to discover novel approaches. As opposed to convergent thinking, which is directed toward a single, correct solution to a problem, divergent thinking demonstrates that there is no one best solution.

Lead Your Team "into the Zone"

Mike Aucoin proposes that we need to be patient, allowing our team members the time to get "into the zone."[7] The premise is this: When we become experienced and skilled at an activity, it becomes internalized. We enter a "zone" that is effortless and often unconscious, like driving a car, typing on a keyboard, or riding a bike. This state is familiar to athletes and musicians. For jazz musicians and improvisational comedians, this is the state where experimentation and spontaneity, and yes, innovation and creativity, come most easily and naturally. A project team can be most creative if its members are *in the zone.* How can project teams make it to the zone? Aucoin suggests these essential elements:

➤ *Practice.* A certain level of competence and skill must come naturally to be in the zone.

➤ *Confidence.* Creativity flourishes when the mind is active but relaxed, when it is not afraid to experiment. A person cannot be in the zone if he or she fears failure or is performing in an environment of mistrust.

➤ *A sense of "professional play."* The individual should approach the task at hand with a sense of curiosity, experimentation, and optimism that is playful even while he or she is performing serious work that leads to breakthroughs.

When faced with significant ambiguity, and the business need or solution has not yet come into view, it is premature to launch an implementation project. Instead, form a small but mighty team of experts to conduct analysis and experimentation. Specifically:

- Recognize that it is imprudent, if not impossible, to move forward without a clear understanding of the business objective.
- Apply professional business analysis techniques to bring the business need and optimal solution into view.
- Use edge-of-chaos management to identify the most valuable solution; delay making decisions until the last responsible moment.
- Become an expert at leading teams to innovative decisions.

- Conduct a formal feasibility study to identify and analyze all potential solution options.
- For cross-functional or enterprise solutions, conduct value-chain analysis.
- Conduct root-cause analysis to ensure that the solution will solve the business problem.

In summary, employ both conventional and adaptive approaches for managing projects with ambiguous business problems, opportunities, or solutions (see Table 12-1).

Managing Ambiguous Projects	
Complexities	**Management Approaches**

· Unclear business problem or opportunity
· Solution difficult to define
· Unclear business objectives
· Unclear solution feasibility
· Stakeholders difficult to identify
· Unclear dependencies/interrelationships
· Unclear project boundaries
· Unclear scope
· Unknown unknowns
	Adaptive
	· Focus on clear business objectives
	· Establish "innovation teams"
	· Apply edge-of-chaos management
	· Guide the group to creative decisions
	· Adopt professional business analysis practices
	  – Feasibility analysis
	  – Root-cause analysis
	  – Value-chain analysis
	  – Business case development
	· Use techniques that foster creativity
	· Build a team that is "in the zone"
	Conventional
	· Establish clear business objectives
	· Conduct project risk analysis

TABLE 12-1. Approaches for Managing Projects with Ambiguous Business Problems, Opportunities, or Solutions

NOTES

1. Jim Johnson, *My Life is Failure: 100 Things You Should Know to be a Successful Project Leader* (West Yarmouth, MA: The Standish Group International, 2006), 6.
2. Kathleen B. Hass, *The Business Analyst as Strategist* (Vienna, VA: Management Concepts, Inc., 2008).

3. The Royal Academy of Engineering, "The Challenges of Complex IT Projects," (April 2004). Online at http://www.raeng.org.uk/news/publications/list/reports/Complex_IT_Projects.pdf (accessed March 2008).

4. Lev Virine and Michael Trumper, *Project Decisions: The Art and Science* (Vienna, VA: Management Concepts, 2008), 7–8.

5. M.E. Porter, *Competitive Advantage* (New York: Free Press, 1985), 39–44.

6. B. Michael Aucoin, *Right-Brain Project Management: A Complementary Approach* (Vienna, VA: Management Concepts, 2007), 93–112.

7. Ibid., 264, 265.

CHAPTER 13

Applying Complexity Thinking to Projects with Poorly Understood, Volatile Requirements

Complexity Dimensions	Project Profile		
	Independent	**Moderately Complex**	**Highly Complex**
Requirements Volatility and Risk	• Strong customer/user support • Basic requirements are understood, straightforward, and stable	• Adequate customer/user support • Basic requirements are understood, but are expected to change • Moderately complex functionality	• Inadequate customer/user support • Requirements are poorly understood, volatile, and largely undefined • Highly complex functionality

P roject complexity ensues when requirements are unstable and poorly understood, functionality is likely to be complex, or customer/user support is insufficient. In this chapter we explore the elements that make dynamic, poorly understood requirements complex and recommend management techniques that the project leader and team can use to manage the resulting complexities.

WHAT MAKES DYNAMIC, POORLY UNDERSTOOD REQUIREMENTS COMPLEX?

> *"Individual requirements are rarely complex in themselves; it is the relationships and interdependencies between them that result in complexity—so it is these that need to be spotted and managed."*
>
> —DAN ROSSNER, PA CONSULTING GROUP

Defining and managing requirements is hard—*very hard*—for many reasons. The complexity of the requirements management effort is rooted in widespread deficiencies in requirements practices, inadequate involvement by key stakeholders, and numerous interdependencies among individual requirements.

DEFICIENT REQUIREMENTS PRACTICES

> *"In the U.S. alone, up to 60 percent of software developers are involved in fixing errors."*
>
> —CAPERS JONES
> SOFTWARE PRODUCTIVITY RESEARCH

Dan Rossner of PA Consulting Group, a leading management, systems, and technology consulting firm, tells us that requirements flaws most often lurk in complex projects when the following conditions are present:[1]

➤ Requirements are not visualized or communicated in the right way to the right audience.

➤ The same level of detail is applied to all requirements, regardless of the need.

➤ A disproportionate amount of effort is expended managing the requirements *process* rather than managing the requirements themselves throughout the life of the project.

INSUFFICIENT STAKEHOLDER INVOLVEMENT

It is often extremely difficult to get the appropriate stakeholders engaged and committed to help define, progressively elaborate, and manage requirements throughout the project. After all, they have a business to run; business stakeholders often believe that requirements definition is the responsibility of the project team, not the business leaders.

REQUIREMENTS INTERDEPENDENCIES

It is the relationships and interdependencies between requirements—far more than the requirements themselves—that result in complexity. And then there are the changes. Requirements are dynamic, changing as they are progressively elaborated and more information is discovered, and changing as the business transforms. Managing these changes adds another layer of complexity.

CASE STUDY: POORLY UNDERSTOOD, VOLATILE REQUIREMENTS
COTS ERP System Acquisition and Deployment

For an example of poorly understood, volatile requirements, we look to the project undertaken by a leading vendor to provide a major enterprise requirements planning (ERP) software solution for a government agency. The vendor promised to provide commercial-off-the-shelf (COTS) ERP solutions for finance, human capital management, customer relationship management, and business intelligence applications tailored to the needs of the government sector. The vendor also committed to provide best-in-class service and support.

The first module was to be the human capital management application. The management team of the human resource (HR) directorate committed to adopting the management practices embedded within the system rather than making wholesale changes to the purchased application. An implementation team was formed consisting of vendor representatives and key members of the HR group; together they developed a project plan and budget that assumed little or no customization. The team worked diligently for many months to prepare for the new system, installing and testing the system and training the IT team to provide maintenance and support. This initial effort took about 18 months and cost almost $20 million.

As preparation for the installation and deployment of the new system proceeded, the organization underwent a major reorganization and many members of the HR directorate management team were replaced. During user training and acceptance testing, it became apparent that the system did not support the current HR practices, yet the new management team was not prepared to change "the way things have always been done around here." The project team had neglected to continually validate requirements with the business at key decision points and was therefore unaware of the change in expectations. The result was a failed and canceled project.

HOW TO MANAGE POORLY UNDERSTOOD, UNSTABLE REQUIREMENTS

Several strategies can be effective in managing requirements complexity. We recommend conducting rigorous enterprise analysis, establishing a framework for managing requirements complexity, and adopting agile requirements analysis and solution development techniques.

RIGOROUS ENTERPRISE ANALYSIS

Rigorous enterprise analysis should be performed prior to project funding and before the project leader seeks executive approval for the project scope and approach.

Complete Rigorous Analysis Prior to Project Funding

Most organizations do not conduct a complete and thorough analysis of the area of the enterprise undergoing change prior to funding significant business projects. As a result, many projects get underway with unclear expectations and a poor understanding of the business need.

A thorough analysis of the enterprise prior to project initiation may include vision and business planning, problem structuring, stakeholder and purpose analysis, behavior modeling, value modeling, solution structuring, and feasibility analysis. Through these activities the business can define the problem or opportunity, select and define the solution concept, and prepare the business case.

If these activities have not been performed prior to project initiation, we recommend that the project leader secure the help of a core team of experts from the business and technical communities. The requirements definition that is completed after project initiation will still be challenging, but it will be significantly easier and less risky.

Secure Executive Approval for the Project Scope and Approach

A complex project needs strong executive support. If the initiative does not have a strong and committed sponsor who is responsible for delivering the business benefits promised in the business case, recruit one. Share the results of the enterprise analysis activities captured in the business case with the sponsor. Make sure the initiative is prioritized, approved, funded, and strategically important to both the sponsor and the enterprise.

A FRAMEWORK FOR MANAGING REQUIREMENTS COMPLEXITY

For complex projects, we strongly suggest establishing a framework for managing requirements complexity. Establishing this framework involves several key steps:

➤ Establish requirements integration teams

➤ Recruit a professional business analyst

➤ Insist on adequate customer, end-user, and technical involvement

➤ Establish a requirements knowledge management system.

Establish Requirements Integration Teams

Set up a *requirements integration team* to manage requirements relationships and interdependencies. Identify boundaries and ensure that each team knows its area of responsibility and is aware of the areas of overlap. For these teams to be successful, they must have expert knowledge of the business domain, IT, and the requirements definition and management process.

Recruit a Professional Business Analyst

Critical, complex projects need a full-time, senior business analyst (BA) and will likely need a business analysis team to elicit, analyze, specify, validate, and manage requirements. Secure the involvement of a full-time, senior BA to lead the requirements activities and manage the requirements integration teams. It takes a great deal of knowledge about the business and experience managing requirements to strike the right balance between too much and too little detail, so look for experience. Secure the help of a Certified Business Analyst Professional qualified by the International Institute of Business Analysis (IIBA; see www.theiiba.org).

Ensure that the BA updates the business case at key decision points to validate that the investment in the project is still warranted. Review the updated business case and project documents with the executive sponsor to secure funding for the next iteration/phase of the project.

Insist on Adequate Customer, End-User, and Technical Involvement

Secure key resources from the relevant business and technical organizations to participate as full-fledged members of each requirements integration team for the life of the project. With the help of the business and technical representatives, continually validate the team boundaries and ensure that each team knows its area of responsibility and the dependencies it must manage. Require each team to document and manage interrelationships with requirements outside its responsibility, as well as interrelationships between the requirements the team owns. Assign each requirements integration team responsibility for tracing its requirements throughout design, construction, and test work products, as well as for integrating its requirements into the overall solution.

Establish a Requirements Knowledge Management System

Requirements come in many forms, for example, a requirement specification, model, or process description. In addition, requirements are embedded in many business artifacts: plans, goals, objectives, executive presentations, a document or a section of a document, policies, procedures, business rules, or even email verbiage. Establish a knowledge management system that links requirements to their relevant business source documents.

AGILE METHODS

The agile movement is flourishing because requirements are so volatile and so difficult to manage. To reduce requirements complexity, we recommend several agile approaches:

➤ Agile, iterative requirements definition and analysis techniques

➤ Sophisticated requirements visualization techniques

➤ Test-driven requirements definition techniques

➤ Incremental solution development techniques.

The world of agile analysis challenges business analysts to become the communications mentors and coaches of project teams when needed and to get out of the way when appropriate. To do this, one of the tenets of agile methodology must be followed: active stakeholder participation throughout the project life cycle. The focus changes from working to find out what customers want to helping them determine what they want and need.

The obvious enabler to active stakeholder participation is co-location of the business and technical teams. However, the business community cannot always free critical resources to work with the development team on a full-time basis. In this case, the business analyst conducts interviews and workshops with the business community in its own environment, with key members of the development team present to hear "the voice of the customer."

SCOTT AMBLER
Agile Analysis[2]

As presented by Scott Ambler, agile analysis is a highly iterative and incremental process whereby developers and project stakeholders actively work together to understand the domain, identify what needs to be built, estimate functionality, prioritize the functionality, and (optionally) produce artifacts that are just barely good enough. Ambler describes the characteristics of agile analysis as follows:

- *Communication-rich.* Analysis is communication-rich, valuing face-to-face meetings and teleconferencing over documentation and email.
- *Highly iterative.* Agile analysis is highly iterative. Analysis and design activities are dependent on each other and in practice are matured in an iterative manner. Indeed, since estimating is part of analysis, it is impossible to estimate the cost of a solution without knowing the solution design.
- *Constant feedback.* Agile analysis is highly incremental, so that components of the solution can be implemented for customer feedback before committing to further investment in development. Hence, estimation and prioritization of requirements in increments are essential. This approach facilitates tradeoff analysis and critical decision-making on the part of the customer.
- *Just enough.* Agile analysis follows the premise that good is good enough. It is the art of applying just the right amount of rigor—no more and no less.

Use Agile, Iterative Requirements Definition and Analysis Techniques

Avoid spending too much time early in the project striving to define requirements in detail. Use the 80/20 rule to uncover 80 percent of requirements at the start of the project. Change happens, so we need to *just get over it.* It is futile to try to develop and freeze requirements and then limit changes. Expect, plan for, and welcome changes that add value to the business. It is simply a fact that new information about requirements will be discovered in the course of the project.

Reduce the cost of change by using incremental development methods. Define requirements and early design concurrently and collaboratively. Know what needs to be done at the front end to understand the *basic requirements*; the goal is that these will become firm, with little chance of changing (see the discussion of firm basic requirements in Chapter 9).

This approach requires a paradigm shift from trying to define detailed requirements up front to letting requirements emerge through more creative, adaptive, and agile approaches. The focus is not on managing changes to requirements, but rather on managing requirements throughout the project life cycle.

JIM JOHNSON
Lessons Learned from the Agile Community[3]

Jim Johnson offers some advice for analyzing requirements:

1. Use an iterative development style; it is the heart and soul of an agile process.
2. Collaborate with team members as part of the agile development process.
3. Follow up with rapid feedback, which promotes quickness and velocity—the cornerstones of agile methods.
4. Recognize that the agile process instills better testing and code quality controls than conventional software development.
5. Consider using a Web-based standard infrastructure as a key component to the agile style.

6. Adopt a policy of no new releases and implement features and functions in a rapid pace on a standard infrastructure.
7. Rethink that old adage about doing risky things first.

Use Sophisticated Requirements Visualization Techniques

The more customers can visualize the solution, the easier it will be for them to validate that all requirements have been satisfied. Create a blueprint (a view or conceptual model) of what the solution will cover. This view will serve as the starting point for scoping the effort and defining the timing of critical and non-critical functionality. The blueprint should depict the business scope in terms of processes and functions and identify the key stakeholders who will interact with the solution. The visual should also depict what the new solution will not handle so that the effort to develop manual procedures can be understood.

Create requirements-understanding models, simulations, and prototypes to make the requirements visual. Develop "a-day-in-the-life" scenarios to help clarify and validate requirements. Communicate, communicate, communicate! Use technology to share information when the team members are geographically separated—for example, video recordings of user operations; webcasts of business vision and rationale for change; and live, interactive usability testing.

Use Test-Driven Requirements Definition Techniques

Requirements that are not testable are not complete. Build the test case before or concurrently with documenting requirements. Sometimes building the test case clarifies the requirement, helps define it, or even changes it.

Use Incremental Solution Development Techniques

Agile development is a highly iterative and incremental process, where developers and project stakeholders actively work together to understand the domain, identify what needs to be built, and prioritize functionality.[4] Use agile development methods when project value is understood; firm basic requirements are clear; the customer participates throughout the project; the customer, designers, and developers are co-located; incremental feature-driven development is possible; and visual documentation (cards on the wall versus formal documentation) is acceptable.

Iteration is the best defense against uncertainty and unpredictability. Use iterative approaches when defining requirements and building systems to manage changes to requirements throughout the life of the project. Determine lessons learned after each iteration with two goals in mind: (1) to drive down the cost of change and (2) to increase innovation and the value of the solution.

In this chapter we first explored the causes of project complexity when requirements are unstable and poorly understood. We then recommended management techniques for you to consider to help you and your team manage the complexities brought about by dynamic, poorly understood requirements. Specifically, we discovered:

- We sometimes cause requirements defects by neglecting to depict and communicate requirements in a way that ensures the various stakeholders can understand them.
- We should not try to define the requirements in detail up front or to apply the same level of detail to all requirements regardless of the need.

- A disproportionate amount of effort is expended managing the requirements process rather than managing the requirements themselves throughout the life of the project. To manage poorly understood requirements, a complete analysis should be performed prior to project funding and the support of a strong executive sponsor should be enlisted.
- A framework for managing requirements complexity that involves requirements integration teams, a professional business analyst, and adequate customer, end-user, and technical involvement should be established.
- A requirements knowledge management system that links requirements to business plans and goals should be established.
- Agile methods should be used to manage change and limit rework; these may include agile, iterative requirements definition and analysis, requirements visualization, test-driven requirements definition, and incremental solution development techniques.

When requirements are expected to be volatile, it is prudent to use both conventional and adaptive project management approaches (Table 13-1).

Managing Projects with Poorly Understood, Volatile Requirements	
Complexities	**Management Approaches**

Requirements alone are not complex; it is the interdependencies and interrelationships that make them complex:
• Inconsistent expectations
• Insufficient/sporadic stakeholder involvement, leading to missed, ambiguous, and incomplete information
• Deficient/inadequate practices, causing defect-laden requirements
• Unknown unknowns
• Requirement complexities:
  – Ambiguity
  – Interdependencies
  – Interrelationships
  – Boundaries
  – Overlaps
  – Inconsistencies
  – Changes
  – Traceability
	Adaptive
	• Use professional business analysis practices
	• Establish requirements integration teams
	• Minimize scope
	• Use agile requirements analysis
	  – Test-driven requirements development
	  – Iteration/incremental development
	  – Visualization/visual control
	• Define at the appropriate level of detail
	• Establish a requirements knowledge management system
	• Communicate the right message to the right audience to continually validate requirements
	Conventional
	• Involve customers/users throughout the project
	• Manage changes

TABLE 13-1. Approach to Managing Projects with Poorly Understood, Volatile Requirements

NOTES

1. Dan Rossner, "Flushing the Requirement Gremlins Out of Complex Programmes: Viewpoint on Complexity," PA Consulting Services Limited (2005). Online at http://www.paconsulting.com/insights/managing_complex_projects/ (accessed February 2008).
2. Scott W. Ambler, "Agile Analysis." Online at www.agilemodeling.com/essays/agileanalysis.htm (accessed March 2008).
3. Jim Johnson, *My Life is Failure: 100 Things You Should Know to be a Successful Project Leader* (West Yarmouth, MA: The Standish Group International, 2006), 8.
4. Scott W. Ambler, "Agile Analysis." Online at www.agilemodeling.com/essays/agileanalysis.htm (accessed March 2008).

CHAPTER 14
Applying Complexity Thinking to High-Visibility Strategic Projects

Complexity Dimensions	Project Profile		
	Independent	**Moderately Complex**	**Highly Complex**
Strategic Importance, Political Implications, Multiple Stakeholders	•Strong executive support •No political implications •Straightforward communications	•Adequate executive support •Some direct impact on mission •Minor political implications •2–3 stakeholder groups •Challenging communication and coordination effort	•Mixed/inadequate executive support •Impact on core mission •Major political implications •Visible at highest levels of the organization •Multiple stakeholder groups with conflicting expectations

omplex projects include highly visible, strategic projects that affect the core mission of the organization, have major political implications, involve multiple stakeholders with conflicting expectations, and require strong executive support. In this chapter we recommend management techniques for you to consider in managing the complexities of these types of high-visibility projects.

WHAT MAKES HIGH-VISIBILITY STRATEGIC PROJECTS COMPLEX?

"Politics is more difficult than physics."

—ALBERT EINSTEIN

Strategic projects are by their very nature politically sensitive. Highly visible projects involve the most powerful and influential people, creating complex organizational and interpersonal situations.

POLITICAL MANEUVERS AND POWER STRUGGLES

Major change almost always destabilizes the existing power structure, prompting unpredictable behaviors at senior levels of the organization. Moreover, every organization has undefined political processes and ever-present power struggles. Political maneuvers can be stifling and overwhelming to a project—if not managed, they can lead to project failure. To survive, much less succeed, project managers and leaders must be aware of and adapt to political events as they occur.

CHANGING STRATEGIES AND EXPECTATIONS

Strategies can shift, causing virtually every aspect of a complex project to change. Project stakeholders often have changing expectations. Executive stakeholder interrelationships create complexity, as do hidden management expectations.

CASE STUDY: HIGHLY VISIBLE STRATEGIC PROJECT
Retail Food and Drug Reengineering Project

During the 1980s and early 1990s, the chairman of a major player in the food and drug industry acquired many regionally owned food and drug stores. He then launched the largest reengineering project in the U.S. retail industry to bring all the regional companies onto one IT system with common business practices. About 100 of the best and brightest young managers were brought together to serve as the reengineering team. An IT staff of about 150 was recruited. A consulting firm was hired to facilitate sessions to determine the future state of the business practices. The same consulting firm committed to modifying its current supply-chain IT system to scale it up for volume and to ensure it met the requirements generated by the reengineering team. The plan was for all the regional companies to become one company and thereby leverage their purchasing power.

The project was visible at the highest levels of the organization: It was about their future. The CFO reported progress to Wall Street on a quarterly basis. The business case was considered sound and promised to return huge profits. Five years into the project, the company was bought out by a competitor. Hundreds of millions of dollars had been spent and nothing was implemented. In addition to the high visibility and strategic nature of the project, many other complexity dimensions contributed to the failure:

- It was too big and took too long.
- The teams were large and geographically dispersed; roles and responsibilities were unclear and volatile.
- The program management team comprised retail executives, not program managers; as a result, issues and risks were raised but not addressed.
- High expectations were publicly announced.

- The "big bang" implementation approach rather than an incremental methodology was followed.
- The project scope was huge and continued to grow.
- The IT solution was selected before the basic requirements were understood.

HOW TO MANAGE HIGH-VISIBILITY STRATEGIC PROJECTS

Managing high-visibility strategic projects effectively involves securing executive support, developing a political management plan, and managing stakeholders.

EXECUTIVE SUPPORT

Strong executive support is crucial to the success of complex projects, particularly if those projects are highly visible. To secure and maintain executive-level support:

➤ Enlist the support of a strong executive sponsor

➤ Establish a steering committee

➤ Focus on business benefits.

Enlist the Support of a Strong Executive Sponsor

Highly visible, strategic projects are likely to have multiple sponsors—the executives whose business units are undergoing transformation, the CIO, and even the CEO. Build a trusting, collaborative relationship with the sponsor(s), seeking mentoring, coaching, and collaboration throughout the project. Begin building a relationship with your project sponsor by discussing the nature and frequency of project communications you will require of each other. By doing so, you will not only build personal rapport but also let your sponsor know that you expect him or her to stay actively engaged in the project.[1]

Establish a Steering Committee

Establish a governance committee consisting of the project sponsor and key members of management who are affected by the project. Build a framework for effective decision-making and project oversight. Consistently focus decision-making on the end goal: realizing the project benefits and achieving strategic goals.

RECIPE FOR PROJECT SUCCESS: THE CHAOS TEN
The Standish Group International, Inc. 2001
#1: Executive Sponsor

Executive support influences the process and progress of a project; lack of executive input can put a project at a severe disadvantage. Current thinking on this topic suggests that the project manager:[2]

1. Have a clear vision for the project that is easily understood
2. Get executive commitment
3. Make fast decisions
4. Have a decision pipeline
5. Focus on executive sponsor process education
6. Use measurements
7. Understand how and why you need to negotiate
8. Have a well-thought-out plan to convince the executive sponsor you are on target and gain his or her support

9. Understand the benefits of a kill switch and why every project should have one

10. Appreciate the merits of celebration—and never take it lightly.

Use the steering committee to address risks, manage change, and set and continually clarify expectations. When bringing issues or risks to the steering committee for resolution, always conduct analyses of options with your core leadership team and be prepared to recommend a solution. Share the options considered, the team's analysis of the feasibility and likelihood of success for each option, and the rationale for your recommendation with the committee. In addition, inform the committee who was involved in the analysis and recommendation effort.

Focus on Business Benefits

Always present your project as central to, and important for, organizational success through the realization of strategic goals. Continually assess the value and organizational impact of the expected project benefits. Ensure that those benefits are achievable, specific, measurable, agreed to, realistic, and time-bound, and document them in the business case. Make certain the project has a business sponsor who is responsible and accountable for the benefits expected from the project. Move from a cost to a revenue focus; concentrate on value, innovation, and risk reduction.

POLITICAL MANAGEMENT STRATEGY

In today's politically charged business environment, project leaders across the globe are beginning to understand the value of assessing the political landscape and establishing a political management strategy. We suggest the following approach:

➤ Create a political management plan

➤ Promote yourself and your project

➤ Leverage the formal authority of functional managers.

Create a Political Management Plan

Every organization operates in a political environment. Individuals engage in political behaviors to acquire or maintain power and influence, resolve conflicts, and achieve organizational or personal objectives. The ability to understand and manage the political environment in organizations is a necessary and vital skill for leaders of complex projects.

To create a political management plan, identify key stakeholder groups and individuals, internal or external to the project. Conduct an analysis to determine who can influence the project and whether they feel positively or negatively about the project. Determine the goals of each key stakeholder. Assess the political environment. Conduct an analysis to identify the strengths, weaknesses, opportunities, and threats (SWOT) affecting your project. Define problems, solutions, and action plans to take advantage of positive influences and to neutralize negative ones. Ask your core team members to do the same. Analyze the results in a collaborative team forum[3] using a stakeholder analysis worksheet (see Table 14-1 for an example).

Stakeholders (Individuals or Groups)	Involvement/ Role	Priorities/ Concerns	Level of Support Needed 1 = their support is not necessary now 2 = helpful to have their support 3 = critically important to have their support	Existing Support + = actively supports the project 0 = neutral to the project – = opposes the project and may work against it ? = level of support unknown	Influence Strategy
Client #1	Major client	Quality CM Discipline On-time delivery	3 Need to fully understand requirements and expectations	+	We have established a positive collaborative relationship with the new program manager. We constantly strive to be easy to work with and provide high quality at low cost.

TABLE 14-1. Stakeholder Analysis Worksheet

Promote Yourself and Your Project

A project manager's power usually derives more from positive relationships than from a formal position of authority in the organizational hierarchy. In essence, the more highly you are regarded, the more personal power you have. People who are held in high regard are those who are considered to be experts in the business domain, possess current and relevant information, are well connected, and are viewed as indispensable.

Find ways to promote yourself and your project. To do so, you must be genuine, competent, and credible. Become visible; do not spend the bulk of your day behind your desk. Make your contributions and efforts across the stakeholder community visible. Invisible efforts and contributions carry no political value.[4]

Leverage the Formal Authority of Functional Managers

Meet often with the functional managers of your project team members and get their approval to provide input to the team members' performance reviews. Also meet with each team member and his or her manager to agree on the amount of time the team member will devote to your project. You may want to leave this meeting with a written agreement between you, the team member, and the manager.[5]

STAKEHOLDER MANAGEMENT

> *"Life is largely a matter of expectations."*
>
> —HORACE (65–8 BC)

Managing the multiple stakeholders involved in a strategic project can be daunting. After identifying key stakeholders and creating your political management plan, be sure to:

➤ Establish positive relationships with key stakeholders

➤ Involve customers and users in every aspect of the project

➤ Establish and manage virtual alliances

➤ Establish and manage expectations.

Establish Positive Relationships with Key Stakeholders

Consider the following stakeholder management strategies presented by Brian Irwin in his book, *Managing Politics and Conflict in Projects*.[6]

➤ Call (do not email) the most critical stakeholders who are allies for your project. Discuss the project with them, asking them how they prefer to be kept informed and how often. Document their responses and schedule stakeholder check-in dates on your calendar.

➤ Record the names of the people you come into contact with during a typical day or week. Note their personal work styles and how they interact with each other. At the end of each week, review these notes. The next time you interact with each person, recall their personal work style and try to adopt and match it as closely as possible. If you experience or witness a poor relationship within your team, engage the individuals and discuss the situation openly. But remember that you cannot enhance a relationship if one is not yet built or if the existing relationship is damaged.

➤ Carefully observe the interactions of team members during project team meetings, particularly if you hold leadership team meetings. Undoubtedly there will be some who always speak up and others who sit quietly on the sidelines. Don't make the mistake of believing that those speaking have more power and influence than others. Interview the team members to get a better understanding of their professional networks and how they relate to others. Individuals with a wide personal and professional network are often well connected to what's going on in their environment and are therefore able to get things done quickly. Make note of who they are and talk to them frequently to help expand your network.

➤ Engage your political adversaries in discussion, however uncomfortable, to turn them into allies. If you both have positive intentions, the meeting should go a long way toward building a collaborative relationship. Focus on discovering shared objectives.

Involve Customers and Users in Every Aspect of the Project

Do not be tempted to diminish user involvement after the initial requirements elicitation activities are complete. As the project unfolds, user concerns and issues mature and change, often requiring refinements to requirements. Keep a constant pulse on user opinions and concerns. Promote opportunities for user feedback often throughout the project.

RECIPE FOR PROJECT SUCCESS: THE CHAOS TEN
The Standish Group International, Inc. 2001
#2: User Involvement

The number one contributor to project success is user involvement. Conversely, lack of user involvement is the number one reason for project failure. Even when delivered on time and on budget, a project can fail if it does not meet users' needs or expectations. The research and thinking on this subject can be summarized as follows:[7]

1. Correctly identify the proper user.
2. Develop and maintain a quality relationship with the user and user groups.
3. Create and maintain a platform for communications to establish and maintain a quality relationship with users.
4. Demonstrate results and understand why it is important to do so.
5. Educate users on the project management process and what their roles and responsibilities are within that process.

6. Consider user feedback and consensus.

7. Identify and recruit an evangelist, someone to promote your project.

8. Show why and how to conduct primary research.

9. Show respect for users.

10. Focus on real user needs.

Establish and Manage Virtual Alliances

Strategic projects involve alliances with suppliers, customers, key political groups, regulatory entities, and even competitors. When seeking out partners, look for the best-in-class competencies to build high-quality, specific products or services in the shortest period of time. You and your leadership team should direct considerable time and effort to fostering alliances with external partners.

Establish and Manage Expectations

In addition to meeting requirements, a successful project manager understands, sets, continually refines, and meets the expectations of stakeholders. The sources of those expectations take many forms: informal conversations, emails, requirements, political climate, cultural norms, promises and commitments you and your team members have made, and offhand remarks made at meetings or in the hallway. And then there are the unspoken expectations—those you may never discover unless you proactively instigate discussions about expectations with all key stakeholders.

According to Albert J. Cacace in his article *Managing Expectations: The Missing Process,* "The level of effort you put into managing each expectation should be proportional to its complexity, its visibility, the bureaucracy involved, number of stakeholders, the risks of failure, and many other considerations. . . ."[8] Expectations are compounded and made complex by the interdependencies between them. Identify expectations, recognize inter- dependencies, and clarify both early in the project. Then, devote effort to managing expectations throughout the project.

Executive support is an essential ingredient in managing complex strate- gic projects effectively. Without executive support, you are setting yourself up for almost certain failure. Enlist the support of an executive sponsor and work diligently to establish a strong, positive relationship with him or her. In addition, establish a project steering committee and an effective decision- making process.

The project leader should also:

- Continually focus on business benefits, and make virtually every decision based on how it will impact the value the project is expected to bring to the organization.

- Establish a political management plan to build upon the support you have and to neutralize resistance to your project success. Learn to promote yourself and your project. Build strong relationships with the functional managers of your team members and leverage their formal authority.

- Devote considerable time and effort to establishing and maintaining positive relationships with key stakeholders and understanding and managing their expectations.

Politically sensitive projects are rife with pitfalls. Use a balanced combina- tion of adaptive and conventional management approaches to increase the likelihood of success (see Table 14-2).

Managing Politically Sensitive Strategic Projects	
Complexities	**Management Approaches**

Constant change caused by:
• Political maneuvers
• Power struggles
• Changing strategies
• Changing expectations
• Inconsistent expectations
• Multiple stakeholder group interrelationships
• Political sensitivity
	Adaptive
	• Establish a political management strategy and plan
	• Establish an executive steering committee with effective decision-making
	• Focus on networking, relationship-building
	• Seek a mentor and coach
	• Manage customer relationships
	• Become a public relations expert:
	  – Promote project
	  – Promote self
	• Focus on business benefits
	• Manage virtual alliances
	• Involve customers and users in every aspect of the project
	• Leverage the authority of the functional managers
	Conventional
	• Establish strong executive sponsorship and executive oversight
	• Devote considerable attention to managing stakeholders and their expectations

TABLE 14-2. Approaches for Managing Politically Sensitive Strategic Projects

NOTES

1. Brian Irwin, *Managing Politics and Conflict in Projects* (Vienna, VA: Management Concepts, 2008), 13.
2. Jim Johnson, *My Life is Failure: 100 Things You Should Know to be a Successful Project Leader* (West Yarmouth, MA: The Standish Group International, 2006), 5.
3. Brian Irwin, *Managing Politics and Conflict in Projects* (Vienna, VA: Management Concepts, 2008), 160.
4. Ibid., 37.
5. Ibid., 13.
6. Ibid., 81, 143, 160.
7. Jim Johnson, *My Life is Failure: 100 Things You Should Know to be a Successful Project Leader* (West Yarmouth, MA: The Standish Group International, 2006), 5.
8. Albert J. Cacace, "Managing Expectations, The Missing Process," *ISSIG Review* (2007), vol. 11, no. 2.

CHAPTER 15

Applying Complexity Thinking to Large-Scale Change Initiatives

Complexity Dimensions	Project Profile		
	Independent	**Moderately Complex**	**Highly Complex**
Level of Organizational Change	• Impacts a single business unit, one familiar business process, and one IT system	• Impacts 2–3 somewhat familiar business units, processes, and IT systems	• Large-scale organizational change that impacts the enterprise • Spans functional groups or agencies • Shifts or transforms the organization • Impacts many business processes and IT systems
Level of Commercial Change	• Minor changes to existing commercial approach	• Enhancements to existing commercial practices	• Ground-breaking commercial practices

P rojects involving large-scale organizational change that impacts business units across the enterprise, shifts or transforms the organization, involves many business processes and IT systems, and may require groundbreaking commercial practices are inherently complex. Appropriate adaptive and conventional management techniques will help you and your team manage the complexities brought about by large-scale transformative change.

WHAT MAKES LARGE-SCALE CHANGE PROJECTS COMPLEX?

"The pressure on organizations to change will only increase over the next decades. Yet the methods managers have used in an attempt to transform their companies into stronger competitors—total quality management, reengineering, right sizing, restructuring, cultural change, and turnarounds—routinely fall short."

—JOHN P. KOTTER, HARVARD BUSINESS SCHOOL PROFESSOR

Twenty-first century large-scale organizational change usually involves new technologies, mergers and acquisitions, restructurings, new strategies, cultural transformation, globalization, new partnerships, or new business practices. Handling change well can mean the difference between the success and failure of a project, and consequently, of an organization. Complexities usually center on resistance to change, the unpredictable emotional responses to change, and errors common to organizational change efforts that fail to address team members' emotional health. In addition, a project that involves the implementation of groundbreaking commercial practices or a new-to-the-world product is rife with many different aspects of complexity.

RESISTANCE TO CHANGE

Large-scale organizational change forces the people within the organization to adjust their behaviors to the changing business environment. Most of us naturally resist change. If we have mastered our current job, we are comfortable with the way things are and we are resentful of imposed change.

Complexity arises when people begin to react to the change in unpredictable ways. Changes to roles, responsibilities, business processes, desktop tools, and IT systems inevitably cause anxiety, concern, tension, and therefore reactions that are likely to be negative and resistant.

EMOTIONAL RESPONSES TO CHANGE

John P. Kotter, the Konosuke Matsushita Professor of Leadership, Emeritus, at Harvard Business School, is perhaps *the* leading expert on successful organizational transformation. Kotter tells us that peoples' emotions undermine change. Anger, pride, arrogance, cynicism, exhaustion, insecurity, and anxiety are common human responses to change. These emotions must be acknowledged and dealt with if the change effort is to be successful.

COMMON CHANGE MANAGEMENT MISTAKES

Kotter identifies eight mistakes common to organizational changes efforts, all of which fail to address peoples' emotional health. These mistakes involve interrelationships, interdependencies, and unintended consequences:[1]

➤ Allowing too much complacency

➤ Failing to create a sufficiently powerful guiding coalition

➤ Underestimating the power of vision

➤ Undercommunicating the vision

➤ Permitting obstacles to block the new vision

➤ Failing to create short-term wins

➤ Declaring victory too soon

➤ Neglecting to anchor changes firmly in the corporate culture.

The result of these errors is obvious: failure to achieve strategic goals, which often results in a diminished position in the marketplace—not to mention the pain felt by nearly every member of the organization touched by the change.

CASE STUDY: NEW-TO-THE-WORLD PRODUCT
The Segway Personal Transportation System

The Segway Personal Transporter (PT) was expected to revolutionize the way people traveled in big cities. Advance interest in the product was high: People in the technology industry thought it might create as big a revolution as the PC. With expectations heightening monthly, the development team geared up for mass production. However, the invention experienced technical problems that led to several recalls, and demand for the product has been disappointing.

"Changing the world isn't easy. It's a lesson Dean Kamen, the guy who invented the Segway 'personal transporter,' has learned the hard way. When he unveiled his self-balancing, battery-powered technological marvel (it seems a sin to call it a scooter) in 2001, Kamen predicted that cities would in the future banish cars from their congested hearts, and wildly popular Segways would fill downtown pavements. Or maybe not. That scenario isn't even remotely likely today. And Kamen, who chairs Segway's board, has been forced to adjust his vision. 'We didn't realize that although technology moves very quickly, people's mindset changes very slowly,' he says. 'People are very cautious, especially when it comes to the big issues.'"[2]

HOW TO MANAGE LARGE-SCALE CHANGE INITIATIVES

*"People change what they do less because they are given analysis that shifts their **thinking** than because they are shown a truth that influences their **feelings**. We see, we feel, we change."*

—John P. Kotter, Harvard Business School Professor

To manage large-scale organizational change initiatives, we suggest the project leader use a proven, research-based change management framework and foster internal motivation to change. For initiatives that involve groundbreaking commercial practices or first-time products, scrupulous industry analysis, prototyping, and a thorough investigation of external constraints may also be required.

CHANGE MANAGEMENT FRAMEWORK

As we have learned, businesses are complex adaptive systems operating within a larger complex adaptive system, the global economy. Organizations must continually adapt to changes in their environment for their very survival. Organizations that handle transformational change well will be the winners; those that simply focus on incremental improvements will be left in their dust.

If your project involves transformational change, you need to look at yourself as much more than a project manager; you must become an expert leader of organizational change. For starters, delve into books by the organizational change experts, such as Kotter's *The Heart of Change*. Kotter, who has developed a highly respected research-based approach to successful organizational transformation, contends that "Successful large-scale change is a complex affair that happens in eight stages:"[3]

1. *Create a sense of urgency.* After identifying key stakeholders and developing a political management strategy, work with stakeholder groups to reduce complacency, fear, and anger over the change and to increase their sense of urgency.

2. *Build the guiding team.* Using some of the same techniques as in managing project and organizational politics, build a team of supporters who have the credibility, skills, connections, reputations, and formal authority to provide the necessary leadership for the transformation.

3. *Get the vision right.* Use the guiding team to develop a clear, simple, compelling vision and a set of strategies to achieve the vision.

4. *Communicate for buy-in.* Execute a simple, straightforward communication plan using forceful and convincing messages sent through many channels. Use the guiding team to promote the vision whenever possible.

5. *Empower action.* Use the guiding team to remove barriers to change, including disempowering management styles, outmoded business processes, and inadequate information.

6. *Deliver short-term wins.* Wins create enthusiasm and momentum. Plan the delivery of short-term wins early and often to gain credibility and positive responses to your project.

7. *Don't let up.* Build on the momentum of short-term wins to make wave after wave of change.

8. *Make change stick.* The goal is to make the change part of the organizational culture—that is, embedded in common behaviors and shared values. This requires consistency of actions over a sufficient period of time for the change to become institutionalized.

CASE STUDY: LARGE-SCALE ORGANIZATIONAL CHANGE
K-12 Public School District
Transformation Program

A large, diverse public school system in the eastern United States is undertaking an exciting school improvement program. The district comprises nearly 175,000 students in almost 200 schools. Performance reports indicated that the school system was doing a quality job educating its students. Yet, there was a strong belief that the system was preparing students to succeed in the 20th century . . . not the 21st century. In response, the Board of Education imposed three new student achievement goals in the areas of academics, essential life skills, and responsibility to the community. The overarching goal is to prepare students for the 21st century challenges of living and working in a global economy.

The district leadership team subdivided the three goals into multiple objectives; the team then decomposed the objectives into more than 30 transformational projects. The objectives are impressive, e.g., students will graduate from high school able to communicate in at least two languages, they will understand the interrelationship and interdependence of the countries and cultures of the world, and they will be able to use technology to apply knowledge and foster creativity.

While the individual projects do not appear to be overly complex, the organizational change effort—implementing major change in nearly 200 schools within three to five years—is immensely complex and will require a sophisticated understanding of how to bring about large-scale organizational change. The district leadership team understands the challenge and is making every effort to increase readiness for change and to prepare the school administration, the teaching staff, parents, students, and the community at large to support and help lead the change effort.

INTERNAL MOTIVATION TO CHANGE

Internal motivation to change comes about through a decision based on the merits of the change. In contrast, external motivation to change is created through incentives such as rewards or punishments. Individuals often resist external change, at least until they internalize the motivation based on the benefits they perceive they will realize as a result of the change.[4]

Clearly, then, you should build relationships with the most influential individuals and work to convince them that your project will bring about change that will benefit them. It is often said that we vote for a candidate for office based on emotion rather than the candidate's policy positions. The same is true of support for change; we welcome change if we internalize emotionally the "goodness" of the change. The 2008 presidential election process provides a timely example. U.S. Senator Barack Obama was able to inspire many Americans to believe that the country needs change based on the merits of the change. By eliciting an emotional response, he drew record crowds of supporters and was likened to a rock star during his primary bid for the Democratic Party candidacy.

GROUNDBREAKING COMMERCIAL PRACTICES

A project that involves the implementation of groundbreaking commercial practices or a new-to-the-world product is rife with many different aspects of complexity. Scrupulous industry analysis is required to develop a new business strategy. Prototyping may be necessary to obtain market feedback. In addition, the external constraints that governmental codes and regulations may impose should be investigated thoroughly.

Conduct Rigorous Industry Analysis

Michael E. Porter, Harvard Business School professor, has developed a framework for analysis when pursuing a revolutionary commercial venture.[5] Porter's framework comprises five forces that help assess the competitive environment and thus determine the viability of an endeavor. An analysis of these five forces is also appropriate when a change occurs in any one of them, as this may drive change to an organization's current commercial practices. Porter's widely known and used framework consists of the following forces:

➤ *Threat of substitute products,* which may lead to buyers switching to competitors if prices increase or satisfaction decreases

➤ *Threat of established rivals,* which includes considerations such as the intensity and number of competitors

➤ *Threat of new entrants,* which will impact profitability forecasts

➤ *Bargaining power of suppliers,* which may lead to exorbitant prices or scarcity of materials

➤ *Bargaining power of customers,* which may put the company under pressure to reduce prices or increase quality.

Ideally, this analysis is performed before project launch. Regardless, the project team must continue the analysis throughout the course of the project, keeping a pulse on the competitive environment; potential customers and suppliers; and the influences of government regulations, the media, and the public.

Conduct Prototyping to Obtain Market Feedback

If the product is truly new, market data may be nonexistent or unreliable. Rapid prototyping will therefore be necessary to obtain market feedback.

This situation calls for late requirements freeze. Product definition will occur iteratively, based on intuition and trial and error. In addition, creating market demand for a groundbreaking new product may require extensive customer education.[6]

Investigate Commercial Practices Rules and Regulations

Compliance with governmental codes and regulations often poses significant constraints when embarking on groundbreaking commercial practices. Concerns include patents, intellectual property issues, and codes and regulations set by local, state, federal, and international governments. Governments issue directives and establish regulations for many reasons:

➤ To enhance consumer rights

➤ To protect consumer health and safety

➤ To prevent exploitation of vulnerable consumers, e.g., children

➤ To make it easier for business to carry out global transactions

➤ To outlaw unwanted practices, e.g., misleading and aggressive marketing.

Commercial practice rules are usually regulated by government agencies. Examples of regulations include the *Code of Federal Regulations,* Title 16: Commercial Practices, and the Government Accountability Office's *Leading Commercial Practices for Outsourcing of IT Services.* The rules and regulations are enforced by national consumer protection authorities and the courts, such as the U.S. Federal Trade Commission and the Consumer Product Safety Commission.

Before embarking on a project to develop new commercial practices or products, be sure to perform the appropriate due diligence by carefully and thoroughly examining and assessing the commercial environment and regulatory constraints. The goal should be to alleviate unknowns, risks, and dependencies prior to launching the new commercial effort.

Much of the complexity of projects involving large-scale organizational change that impacts business units across the enterprise arises from the unpredictable, emotional behaviors of individuals in the organization as they react to and try to resist the change.

To manage the complexities brought about by large-scale organizational change, we recommend taking a proven, research-based approach to leading large-scale change that follows a staged framework. It is also important to create internal motivation to remove the natural human instinct to resist change.

Finally, if your project is developing commercial practices that will break new ground, it is essential to undertake significant, comprehensive research and analysis to ensure that those practices are compliant with government codes and regulations.

A thorough understanding of cultural change management is essential to the success of large-scale organizational change. Appropriate adaptive and conventional change management approaches can help the project team address these complexities (Table 15-1).

Managing Large-scale Change Initiatives	
Complexities	**Management Approaches**
• Unpredictable human emotions • Resistance to change, causing anxiety, tension, anger, pride, arrogance, cynicism, exhaustion, insecurity • Complacency and loss of support, leading to isolation of project team • No executive guiding coalition, causing inconsistent management behaviors • Unclear vision; current culture blocks the new vision	**Adaptive** • Establish a cultural change framework • Create a sense of urgency • Build an influential guiding team • Establish a clear, compelling vision • Communicate for buy-in • Empower stakeholders for action • Deliver short-term wins • Use external and internal incentives • Conduct rigorous industry analysis • Prototype new products **Conventional** • Manage dependencies • Conduct research, due diligence, and analysis

TABLE 15-1.   Approaches for Managing Large-Scale Changes Initiatives

NOTES

1.   John P. Kotter, *Leading Change* (Boston: Harvard Business School Press, 1996), 4–16.
2.   Unmesh Kher, "The Segway Riddle," *Time,* August 14, 2006. Online at http://www.time.com/time/business/article/0,8599,1226309,00.html (accessed March 2008).
3.   John P. Kotter, *The Heart of Change* (Boston: Harvard Business School Press, 2002), 33–158.
4.   B. Michael Aucoin, *Right-Brain Project Management: A Complementary Approach* (Vienna, VA: Management Concepts, 2007), 76–77.
5.   M.E. Porter, "How Competitive Forces Shape Strategy," *Harvard Business Review,* March/April 1979.
6.   Peter W. G. Morris and Jeffrey K. Pinto, *The Wiley Guide to Managing Projects* (Hoboken, NJ: John Wiley & Sons, Inc., 2004), 11.

CHAPTER 16

Applying Complexity Thinking to Projects with Significant Risks, Dependencies, and External Constraints

Complexity Dimensions	Project Profile		
	Independent	**Moderately Complex**	**Highly Complex**
Risks, Dependencies, and External Constraints	• Considered low risk • Some external influences • No challenging integration issues • No new or unfamiliar regulatory requirements • No punitive exposure	• Considered moderate risk • Some project objectives are dependent on external factors • Challenging integration effort • Some new regulatory requirements • Acceptable exposure	• Considered high risk • Overall project success depends largely on external factors • Significant integration required • Highly regulated or novel sector • Significant exposure

Complex projects include those that are high risk because they involve multiple dependencies and external factors. Project leaders should pay particular attention to managing risks and uncertainties on these types of projects.

WHAT MAKES PROJECTS WITH SIGNIFICANT RISKS, DEPENDENCIES, AND EXTERNAL CONSTRAINTS COMPLEX?

Large-scale change inevitably involves cross-functional and cross-project dependencies, external constraints, and changes to the external environment that will require adjustments. For regulated industries, failure to comply with ever-changing rules and regulations may create significant exposure. Additional dependencies and constraints that are difficult to identify and manage involve complex behaviors (of humans and systems), reactions to changes, and unintended consequences of interventions. Projects that involve outsourced products, services, or solutions pose risks because control of major deliverables has been delegated to third parties.

Experience has demonstrated that these dependencies and constraints are dynamic and are sometimes difficult to identify. They are likely to change not only throughout the project, but also after the new solution is deployed. These dependencies and constraints need to be identified, owned, and managed by a senior person on the project leadership team.

COMPLEX BEHAVIORS AND REACTIONS TO CHANGES

Because of interdependencies and complex feedback loops, the effects of changes on complex projects are not discrete events that can be studied in isolation. Small changes can combine to produce very complex behaviors that are virtually impossible to predict. For instance, many minor schedule delays may combine to cause a cataclysmic effect. This phenomenon is known as the *butterfly effect*, whereby a small change at one place in a complex system has large effects elsewhere (e.g., a butterfly flapping its wings in Mexico City sets in motion a series of events that leads to a change in the weather in St. Louis).

On a complex project, it is impossible to understand the full effect of an environmental change by looking at individual parts of the system—such as solution components; project team members; customers and users; cost, schedule, and design components; and individual or sets of requirements. As a result, the project team must constantly adapt to changes as they evolve and are recognized.

UNINTENDED CONSEQUENCES OF INTERVENTIONS

As project managers, we are constantly making decisions to change or correct our plans. In a complex project, these interventions don't always have the effect we expect. In fact, they often cause unintended consequences that require additional intervention. The project manager is often unable to recognize, analyze, and control multiple feedback loops.[1] As a result, a cycle of never-ending changes, leading to unpredictable effects, is created. This causes the project team to constantly adapt to events as they are identified.

OUTSOURCED PRODUCTS, SERVICES, OR SOLUTIONS

Outsourcing components of the solution adds significant complexity and risk to projects. "Every outsourced project by definition is a goal-oriented undertaking of multiple tasks, often interdependent in nature, increasingly involving multiple parties, including customer, principal supplier, supply-chain partners (subcontractors), and other third-parties, to develop or provide products, services, or solutions within a given period of time."[2] Project managers relinquish a certain amount of control over their projects when they engage an outsourcing partner, which can lead to a failed project if the outsourcing relationship is not managed appropriately.

CROSS-FUNCTIONAL AND CROSS-PROJECT DEPENDENCIES

Complex projects almost always involve inter-project dependencies that must be managed. These could involve deliverables produced by another project, e.g., the purchase and installation of office space, supplies, and business equipment that are needed to implement a new business solution. In addition, because business processes are horizontal, a change made by one functional group may cause unknown impacts on another functional group. Again, these dependencies need to be identified, owned, and managed by a senior person on the project leadership team.

REGULATORY AND ENVIRONMENTAL CONSTRAINTS

Compliance issues such as those imposed by building codes, environmental tolerance levels, and food and drug safety policies pose potential risks to projects operating within a regulated industry. For projects that are subject to regulatory compliance, it is important for the project leadership team to keep abreast of emerging regulatory issues and be aware of developments that have the potential to lead to government rulemaking. The project team must be able to craft workable solutions before conditions are imposed from outside the project.

INTEGRATION ISSUES

Complex projects almost always involve multiple, intricate integration issues. Integration applies to all components of the solution: process integration, organizational integration and optimization, data integration and normalization, IT solution component integration and application system interfaces, and integration and optimization of technical infrastructure components. Changes to one component of the solution may cause unintended consequences to the integration and operation of others.

CASE STUDY: PROJECT WITH SIGNIFICANT RISKS, DEPENDENCIES, AND CONSTRAINTS
Denver International Airport

Consider the infamous Denver International Airport (DIA) baggage-handling system. The project to build the airport was initiated in 1989. As the project evolved, the management team recognized that the airport opening date was likely to be delayed because of dependency on one high-risk component: the baggage-handling system. Early in the project, the team elected to pursue an innovative approach to baggage-handling that would reduce labor costs. During every test of the system, the technology failed, with disastrous results—baggage and clothing were spread all over the airport.

To protect the opening date, the program team proposed installing an old-fashioned baggage-handling system as a risk mitigation strategy. However, decision-makers disapproved the expenditure for the redundant system. As a result, construction costs of $186 million ballooned at the rate of $1 million a day for months when the airport's opening was delayed by baggage-handling failures. The old-fashioned system was finally installed so the airport could be opened. Only one airline, United Airlines, has used the innovative system, spending tens of millions of dollars over the years for repairs and modifications. In 2005 United elected to pull the plug on the new baggage-handling system and is expected to save $1 million a month in maintenance costs.[3]

In this case, failure to manage the risk of one component of the solution resulted in millions of dollars in cost overruns and lost revenue due to the delay caused to the overall project—the airport opening.

HOW TO MANAGE PROJECTS WITH SIGNIFICANT RISKS, DEPENDENCIES, AND EXTERNAL CONSTRAINTS

To manage high-risk projects with multiple dependencies and external factors, we recommend techniques for managing risks and uncertainties, dependencies and external constraints, and outsourced projects.

RISKS AND UNCERTAINTIES

The concepts of risk and uncertainty are often used interchangeably in the context of complex projects, but it is important to distinguish between them. A risk is defined as "an uncertain event or condition that, if it occurs, has a positive or negative effect on a project's objectives."[4] A risk may or may not occur. In the context of complex projects, an uncertainty, in contrast, is a *present reality.* Complex projects are riddled with uncertainty. Although conventional project management wisdom tells us to resolve all uncertainties before project execution, this is usually not feasible on a complex project. So we must learn how to make progress in the midst of uncertainty.

Risk management involves planning to accommodate future events that may or may not happen. *Uncertainty management* is the proactive effort to make sense of the project and reduce ambiguity in the present.

Managing Risks

Even though the process is well defined in the *PMBOK® Guide* and many other books on the subject,[5] risk management is one of the most neglected aspects of managing complex projects. In fact, most project managers simply do not perform rigorous risk management on their projects. For complex projects, however, risk management is not an option—it is essential. David

Hillson and Peter Simon, in *Practical Project Risk Management: The ATOM Methodology,* note that effective risk management requires four elements:[6]

➤ A supportive organization

➤ Competent people

➤ Appropriate methods, tools, and techniques

➤ A simple, scalable process.

Hillson and Simon present the simple, scalable process they refer to as ATOM (Active Threat and Opportunity Management). They use a project sizing grid not unlike our *Project Complexity Model* to determine how the ATOM methodology should be applied, from light to heavy. For a complex project involving risks, integration issues, dependencies, and interrelationships, their opinion is that *bigger is better*; they recommend applying the *ATOM Process for Large Projects.*[7] We strongly recommend that leaders of complex projects become experts in this approach.

Managing Uncertainties

To manage uncertainty is to make sense of the current situation. Only when we understand the origins of the uncertainty, and attempt to identify patterns, can we determine the appropriate way forward.[8] Sophisticated project leadership teams often use simulation and probability techniques to predict results in uncertain circumstances and to reduce sensitivity to random variability. Simulation techniques allow the project team to explore "what if?" scenarios to attempt to predict the future. Statistical probability analysis helps the team determine the likelihood of an event. Obviously, the high probability of an event occurring that would cause significant negative impacts should be addressed.

Matthew Leitch, an independent consultant and researcher specializing in internal control and risk management, presents a seven-step approach to managing uncertainty in his essay, "The Basics":[9]

1. Identify uncertainties

2. Consider the impact of your uncertainties

3. Consider monitoring and research

4. Consider mitigation and exploitation

5. Clarify alternative future outcomes

6. Make risk-aware plans

7. Design internal control systems.

DEPENDENCIES AND EXTERNAL CONSTRAINTS

Large-scale organizational change alters much about the environment for many different groups across the enterprise. A change in one functional area may have unwanted consequences in another. In addition, a major transformation project is often dependent on key deliverables from other projects currently underway within the organization or from outsourced components of the solution. Our recommendations for managing dependencies and external constraints include:

➤ Identify inter-group and cross-project dependencies

➤ Assign ownership to dependencies

➤ Manage your project in the midst of changes in your IT environment

➤ Use edge-of-chaos management to adapt to changes in the external environment.

Identify Inter-group and Cross-Project Dependencies

The most difficult part of dependency management is identifying the dependencies. Interrelationships across functional groups are often invisible and difficult to identify and define. Business analysis practices that analyze the value chain and develop functional and process models are designed to make these dependencies visible. As the processes and functions change, new dependencies will emerge and existing dependencies might need to adapt. The core project leadership team needs to spend a great deal of time and effort continually monitoring and adapting its dependency management strategy as the organizational changes take place.

Inter-group dependencies might be among people, information exchanges, policies, business rules, functions, processes, or IT application systems—virtually anywhere across the enterprise. As these dependencies are identified, use visualization techniques to literally map the interdependent processes on the wall. Review and refine often as more is learned. Make key decisions with the dependencies in mind.

Assign Ownership to Dependencies

As dependencies and interrelationships are discovered, assign someone from the core leadership team to serve as the *dependency owner* who will interact with the interdependent functional groups or the other project team creating the deliverable. A best practice is for dependency owners to attend meetings of the dependent group or project to demonstrate the importance of the dependency and to monitor its status firsthand.

Manage Your Project in the Midst of Changes in Your IT Organization

Your IT environment may impose new constraints after your project has begun execution. Virtually all large-scale transformation projects involve changes in IT services. It is important to be aware of change initiatives currently underway in your IT group to improve performance. As part of the improvement process, your IT organization may impose new standards or methods that require you to change your project approach.

In her book *Leading Culture Change in Your Software Organization,* Rita Chao Hadden highlights five highly effective conventional project management practices that she contends any project team should use.[10] Following these practices will go a long way in keeping your project on track even if your IT organization is still be immature and your environment is in a state of flux:

➤ Work with your customers to clearly define, validate, prioritize, and agree on requirements and perform change control.

➤ Carefully plan before executing your project, developing specific strategies to address key concerns early in the project.

➤ Track your progress by key work products and deliverables, not just milestones, and take early corrective action. Resolve issues, external dependencies, and risks to closure, escalating proactively.

➤ Perform effective peer reviews for your key work products and deliverables.

➤ Manage your configuration items throughout your project.

Use Edge-of-Chaos Management to Adapt to Changes in the External Environment

In addition to changes in your IT environment, your team is likely to experience events and changes both within and external to your organization that will impact your project. These may include:

➤ Changes to the regulatory environment that constrain your decisions and pose new requirements

➤ Changes in the business environment that pose new interrelationships, dependencies, and perhaps new requirements, such as mergers and acquisitions

➤ Changes in the competitive environment that establish new interrelationships and dependencies, which may also impose new constraints or requirements

➤ Changes in zoning or building codes (for projects that involve construction).

These external constraints and dependencies require vigilance by the core project leadership team to identify, assign ownership, adapt as changes occur, and rigorously manage each constraint or dependency so that it does not hinder progress.

COMPLEX OUTSOURCED PROJECTS

Outsourced projects are by their very nature risky. The project leader and team must direct special attention to ensuring that the outsource partner understands requirements and is amenable to requirements changes as needed. We offer suggestions for establishing positive supplier partnerships, creating an integrated project management team, and establishing a framework for managing outsourced projects.

Establish Positive Supplier Partnerships

Positive supplier partnerships are crucial if we are to adjust as we learn, adapt as our environment changes, and manage project complexities. Seek out suppliers who are focused on quality and who routinely establish positive partnerships with their customers. Together, perform value-chain analysis, from the subcontractors to the prime supplier to your organization, through to the customers of your business. Ensure that all along the way on the value chain, everyone is focused on their requirements and the quality of their products and services. Review and adjust the value-chain processes as the project progresses and learning occurs.

Best practices gleaned from companies that have mastered the art of establishing positive outsourcing partnerships that have led to project success include the following:[11]

1. Clearly define the scope and schedule for your project

2. Evaluate a service provider like you'd hire a full-time employee

3. Look for specific experience fit

4. Don't choose a vendor based solely on price

5. Review portfolios and samples

6. Start small

7. Tie payment to clearly defined project milestones

8. Negotiate ownership of work up front

9. Don't forget about support after the project is complete

10. Get it in writing.

Create an Integrated Project Management Team

Establish a small, integrated "tiger team" consisting of key members of the core program team, the supplier and major subcontractors, and the business.

Involve all parties in the requirements elicitation, analysis, and specification activities so that they share a common understanding of the requirements themselves as well as the requirements management process. Schedule frequent feedback sessions where supplier and subcontractor representatives provide business representatives with prototypes, models, and increments of the solution for their review, feedback, and validation. Manage the suppliers and subcontractors as trusted partners. (See Chapter 10 for additional information on how to lead large, geographically dispersed, culturally diverse project teams.)

Establish a Framework for Managing Outsourced Projects

Managing complex projects becomes even more challenging when it involves coordinating processes, schedules, individuals, and teams around the globe. For an outsourcing partnership of any length or criticality, establish a solid management framework. One such framework involves four layers:[12]

➤ *Governance layer,* consisting of:

  › Offshore development strategy

  › Definition of the working model

  › Articulation, measurement, and monitoring of the service-level agreement

  › Stakeholder management

  › Dispute resolution.

➤ *Management layer,* consisting of:

  › Project management

  › Global team management

> ❯ Appreciation for globalization, outsourcing, offshoring, and internationalization.

➤ *Technical layer,* consisting of roles and responsibilities for:

> ❯ Program and project managers

> ❯ Delivery managers

> ❯ Business development managers

> ❯ Core technical teams, comprising module leaders and developers

> ❯ On-site coordinators.

➤ *Communication layer,* consisting of:

> ❯ Defining communication protocols

> ❯ Communication infrastructure

> ❯ Optimizing time difference.

> On projects that involve multiple dependencies and external constraints, complex behaviors and unintended consequences invariably result from interventions. The project leader and team can adopt certain techniques to manage the complexities brought about by risks, constraints, and dependencies. Specifically, we recommend a combination of adaptive and conventional techniques, including rigorous risk and uncertainty management, ownership and management of internal and external dependencies, and establishment of a framework for managing external partners (Table 16-1).

Managing Projects with Complex Dependencies and External Constraints	
Complexities	**Management Approaches**

• Unpredictable human behaviors
• Unknown dependencies
• Unknown constraints
• Interrelating constraints
• Unpredictable reactions to change and interventions
• Unintended consequences
• Outsourced team dependency
• Cross-functional and cross-project dependencies
• Regulatory issues
• Integration issues
	Adaptive
	• Manage uncertainties
	• Assign owners to dependencies
	• Adapt to new practices
	• Employ edge-of-chaos management
	• Establish a framework for managing external partner dependencies:
	  – Supplier partnerships
	  – Integrated design teams
	  – Governance
	  – Management
	  – Technical
	  – Management
	Conventional
	• Manage risk
	• Conduct contract negotiations
	• Manage contacts

TABLE 16-1. Approaches for Managing Projects with Complex Dependencies and External Constraints

NOTES

1. Terry Williams, "Complexity in Project Management and the Management of Complex Projects," presented at the PMI Research Working Session at the PMI Global Congress North America (October 2007).

2. Gregory A. Garrett, *Managing Complex Outsourced Projects* (Chicago: CCH Incorporated, 2005), 2.

3. Kirk Johnson, "Denver Airport Saw the Future. It Didn't Work" (August 27, 2005). Online at http://www.nytimes.com/2005/08/27/national/27denver.html?ex=1282795200&en=55c1a4d8 ddb7988a&ei=5088&partner=rssnyt&emc=rss (accessed March 2008).

4. Project Management Institute, *A Guide to the Project Management Body of Knowledge, Third Edition* (Newtown Square, PA: Project Management Institute, 2004), 373.

5. Ibid.

6. David Hillson and Peter Simon, *Practical Project Risk Management: The ATOM Methodology* (Vienna, VA: Management Concepts, 2007), 17.

7. Ibid., 149–170.

8. B. Michael Aucoin, *Right-Brain Project Management: A Complementary Approach* (Vienna, VA: Management Concepts, 2007), 140–141.

9. Matthew Leitch, "The Basics," (March 2003) Online at http://www.managedluck.co.uk/basics/index.html (accessed March 2008).

10. Rita Chao Hadden, *Leading Culture Change in Your Software Organization* (Vienna, VA: Management Concepts, 2003), 17–18.

11. Keith R. Crosley, "Top Ten Tips for Outsourcing Success," *About, Inc.* (2008). Online at http://entrepreneurs.about.com/cs/beyondstartup/a/uc041003a.htm (accessed February 2008).

12. Mohan Babu, "Managing and Implementing Outsourced Projects. Using an Offshoring Management Framework," Computerworld Management (2005). Online at http://www.computerworld.com/managementtopics/outsourcing/story/0,10801,107069,00.html?SKC=outsourcing-107069 (accessed February 2008).

CHAPTER 17

Applying Complexity Thinking to Projects with a High Level of IT Complexity

"For every complex problem there is a simple solution. And it is wrong:"

—H. L. Mencken, Journalist and Satirist

Complexity Dimensions	Project Profile		
	Independent	**Moderately Complex**	**Highly Complex**
Level of IT Complexity	• Solution is readily achievable using existing, well-understood technologies • IT complexity is low	• Solution is difficult to achieve or technology is proven but new to the organization • IT complexity and legacy integration are moderate	• Solution requires groundbreaking innovation • Solution is likely to use immature, unproven, or complex technologies provided by outside vendors • IT complexity and legacy integration are high

The development of business solutions with software-rich features supported by innovative technology is a complex venture. Over and over again, we see evidence of IT teams that are working on components of the system; these teams are often unable to manage the dependencies and integration risks, resulting in (1) schedule and cost overruns to fix the issues, (2) defects discovered by the customer in the field, and (3) erosion of the business benefits expected from the new solution. IT organizations are structured so that the hardware and the software components are provided by different technical teams, which can lead to bandwidth, performance, and compatibility issues. With complexity accelerating, far-reaching new managerial techniques, partnerships, and technologies are needed if we are to maintain our economic competitiveness.

WHAT MAKES PROJECTS WITH SIGNIFICANT IT COMPONENTS COMPLEX?

Virtually all projects that involve significant new IT products and services are highly complex. The complexity of IT projects comes in many flavors, both technical and managerial. In addition, the need to build the next generation of IT systems that are agile and easily modified is becoming ever more urgent.

TECHNICAL COMPLEXITIES

IT solutions are technically complex if they involve a widespread collection of applications functioning together to achieve a common mission. Moreover, the use of unproven technology adds significant complexity for the technical team to manage. Solutions that involve multiple products from diverse vendors may not follow the same protocol, causing significant integration issues. Examples of business solutions with significant IT complexity are communications networks and enterprise resource planning applications.

MANAGERIAL COMPLEXITIES

Projects to design and build complex IT solutions are usually accompanied by several other complexity dimensions, including:

➤ Multiple contractors providing components of the solution that must be integrated

➤ A large and diverse project team, with a program office to coordinate subprojects and a large collection of subject matter experts (technical, administrative, finance, legal, etc.)

➤ A central master plan, with separate plans for subprojects

➤ A formal bureaucracy that is highly visible and sensitive to political, environmental, and social issues.

NEED FOR AGILITY

"Most business applications are too inflexible to keep pace with the businesses they support."

—JOHN RYMER AND CONNIE MOORE, FORRESTER

To remain competitive, organizations need flexible, adaptable business solutions and consumer products that rely on embedded IT systems. The business world has recently become well aware that its inflexible business processes and IT business applications form barriers to business agility at every turn. Successful 21st century businesses need to streamline their processes and applications to be nimble, adaptable, and agile if they are to keep pace with changes in the competitive landscape and in customer preferences.

Product-focused businesses make every effort to be seen as leaders in innovation. Undeniably, their future growth and position in their industries hinge on their ability to develop innovative products and services while maintaining the quality and customer satisfaction of their current offerings. Many innovative consumer products are dependent on IT applications: automobiles, cameras, mobile phones, PDAs, iPods, and virtually all household appliances, to name a few. Many of these software-rich products are mobile, so they need to be engineered to be as self-reliant as possible, to adapt to customer preferences, styles, and usage patterns, and to need little in the way of IT support.

Likewise, customer-facing business processes need to be intelligent and adaptive, or customers will simply go to a competitor whose systems are intuitive and easy to use. Unfortunately, our methods for building adaptive IT systems are sadly inadequate. The problem is that the complexity of business solutions and innovative products is growing faster than our ability to devise radical new approaches to replace current software development technologies. In addition, the increasing demand for software-rich safety-critical systems and medical devices means that the stakes are growing ever higher, with the potential for IT system failures having high human costs.[1] Without a doubt, we need to quickly adopt more contemporary IT development approaches.

TECHNIQUES TO HARNESS IT COMPLEXITY FOR COMPETITIVE ADVANTAGE

For the past 20 years, cio.com has produced the "CIO 100," a list of the top CIOs across multiple industries. In 2007, the winners were dubbed *The Transformers* for their contributions to their companies in terms of innovation and increased business value. Companies that strive to harness technology for competitive advantage need ". . . to have IT departments that understand what makes their companies tick and IT leaders who know how to translate visions into actions. . . . This year's CIO 100 Awards honorees understand. They've embraced IT innovation as a tool for transformation, their winning projects motivated by critical business needs and the conviction, backed by solid analysis, that technology-enabled change can create new value. The CIOs at these companies define themselves not as technology suppliers but as facilitators of corporate growth."[2]

Organizations innovate in many different ways, ranging from product innovation to process innovation to customer experience innovation. To design, build, and maintain innovative, adaptive products and business solutions that are dependent on highly complex IT applications, we must understand and account for business strategies as they evolve, customer inclinations as they transform, and the competitive environment as it changes. In addition, we must be able to build and support nested systems within systems, complex business rules, and the intricate feedback loops that are characteristic of software-rich systems.

Jim Highsmith, one of the gurus in the agile project management arena, tells us that today's development teams must strive to adopt the objectives of *reliable innovation:*[3]

➤ *Continuous innovation:* to deliver on current customer requirements

➤ *Product adaptability:* to deliver on future customer requirements

➤ *Reduced delivery schedules:* to meet market windows and improve return on investment

➤ *People and process adaptability:* to respond rapidly to product and business change

➤ *Reliable results:* to support business growth and profitability.

While building software-intensive systems is an engineering specialty all its own, we offer a few promising managerial and technical techniques that are appearing on the horizon.

ADAPTIVE MANAGEMENT APPROACHES

Thought leaders in the IT industry suggest that radical new approaches are required to build complex adaptive products and business solutions. We offer these up-and-coming management approaches to foster innovation and customer empowerment:

➤ Build solutions that empower customers

➤ Establish "skunk works" teams

➤ Exploit the advantages of edge-of-chaos management

➤ Introduce a last-responsible-moment decision-making process

➤ Structure the effort into micro projects

➤ Create communities of practice and diversity of thought

➤ Ensure your IT architect is seasoned

➤ Forge new partnerships

➤ Set up integration teams

➤ Strike the right balance between discipline and agility.

Build Solutions that Empower Customers

To design and build complex adaptive business systems that are responsive to changes in customer preferences and the global marketplace, IT leaders across the landscape are focusing their teams on several concepts: innovation, adaptability, customer empowerment, and revenue generation. IT business solutions are not about cost savings any more; they are about revenue generation and empowering customers to drive the system so that they get what they want, when and how they want it. Forward-thinking, successful CIOs from Washington Mutual, Best Buy, and Hilton Hotels cite three simple yet daunting steps to building solutions that empower the customer:[4]

1. Find out everything you can about the customer.

2. Build a system that anticipates his every wish.

3. Step back, get your own business processes out of the way, and let him do his thing.

To find out everything you can about your customers, conduct extensive research and information-gathering focusing on their preferences, likes, and dislikes. Then put together a creative team to anticipate what customers will want in the future. Since it is impossible to predict the future precisely, it takes lots of experimentation and prototyping to bring into focus a solution that will be adaptable as customer preferences change.

Establish "Skunk Works" Teams

We learn from the 2007 CIO 100 honorees report that innovations most often originate from business leaders or cross-functional teams established to tackle a specific problem or opportunity. Seventy-eight percent of the CIOs surveyed said that IT shares leadership of innovative projects with business sponsors.[5] Establish teams modeled after *skunk works teams* (see Chapter 7), which are semi-autonomous project teams separated from the operations of the larger organization to work on critical, time-sensitive, complex, and sometimes secret projects. This strategy was made famous by a division of Lockheed Martin, the world's largest defense contractor, which achieved great success by fielding autonomous teams to manage complex and sensitive projects.

Exploit the Advantages of Edge-of-Chaos Management

"Profound new solutions can emerge from instability and even from near chaos."

—HUGH CRAIL, PA CONSULTING GROUP

Edge-of-chaos management is also relevant in the context of building innovative products and adaptive business solutions. Encourage your team to operate on the edge of chaos by brainstorming, creating, studying, examining ideas, experimenting, and evaluating flexibility, adaptability, and interdependencies to select the most innovative, revenue-generating, and customer-empowering solution.

In some cases, expert designers will begin to design and develop more than one solution in order to prove which one is truly the most elegant and adaptable. When this approach is used, the outcome can be more innovative and creative than ever imagined. So, again, if your team seems to be operating on the edge of chaos, it might be just the right place to be! (See Chapter 10 for the behaviors and perspectives characteristic of teams operating on the edge of chaos.)

Introduce a Last-Responsible-Moment Decision-Making Process

So how do you know when to wind down experimentation and get down to building something? In *Lean Software Development: An Agile Toolkit*, Mary and Tom Poppendieck[6] describe a technique for making better decisions. They advocate that teams dealing with ambiguity and constant change start development when only partial requirements are known, develop partial solutions in small components iteratively, and build in feedback and learnings after each iteration so that the solution *emerges*. This approach allows for solution design decisions to be made iteratively as more is learned and encourages the development team to delay commitment to a design concept until *the last responsible moment*. Design decisions are deferred until all viable options have been explored as fully as possible. The goal is to increase solution adaptability and customer value.

This approach refrains from making decisions too early, when not much is known and more risk is involved. However, be mindful that if decisions are delayed beyond this point, they are likely to be made by default, which can have highly negative consequences. It is up to the complex project manager to intuitively guide the timing of team decisions.

Structure the Effort into Micro Projects

The Standish Group International predicts that micro projects will dominate the IT landscape in the 21st century. Micro projects are the ultimate in minimization; they last no more than four months, involve no more than four people, and cost around $100,000. As noted, the Standish Group CHAOS research indicates that micro projects are more successful than customary large-scale IT projects.[7]

The many positive aspects of micro projects include the following: Valuable solution components are delivered early and often, learnings occur with each deployment, benefits can be realized immediately, and problems are identified and fixed quickly. However, micro projects also have downsides: It takes considerable effort to manage resources across the many projects, configuration management may be made more difficult, and dependencies between projects are difficult to manage.

Create Communities of Practice and Foster Diversity of Thought

To leverage the diverse expertise needed to build complex adaptive business systems, project leaders often establish an *integrated solution design team* that comprises empowered experts who have clear roles, responsibilities, and authority as well as a common understanding of the project vision. Diversity of core solution design team members is critical for them to come up with the best solution, i.e., one that can react to changes in the environment.

On complex projects, communication is of utmost importance. Within any expert group, a significant amount of unspoken knowledge is held in people's heads. This sometimes vital information may be intuitive, experiential, or judgmental, and it is often context-sensitive. In addition, the information may be difficult to articulate and it is almost never recorded. Establishing formal *communities of practice* to share this knowledge facilitates the emergence of collaborative solutions that are much more innovative than they would be if designed by a single architect.[8]

Ensure Your IT Architect Is Seasoned

The vital role of the IT architect has been woefully underused in the IT world. As a result, there is a shortage of individuals who are skilled and seasoned IT architects—an expertise that is essential when building complex

IT systems. This role is becoming pivotal to complex IT projects because of the extent of technology options (hardware, software, and communications) available today. The job of the architect is not just about IT; it is also about achieving business benefits. The architect has the vision of how the new solution will look when it is put together with business processes, policies, manual procedures, training, and desktop tools, and when personnel are in place to use the new technology.

Strive to recruit a certified IT architect experienced in specifying, designing, implementing, testing, releasing, and driving maintenance of either semi-custom or custom software. Embed the solution architect into the project team from the very beginning, when the solution concept is being defined and lots of experimentation is expected.

> ### ED TITTEL
> ### Technology editor, *Certification Magazine*[9]
> ### IT Architects: Blueprint for a Future Career
>
> An IT architect is an individual who not only understands multiple aspects of information technology from a technical and development or implementation perspective, but who also understands how the proper application and use of IT can help an organization or company meet its goals, improve productivity or profitability and, in general, help organizations work more effectively. Thus, an IT architect brings an understanding of and appreciation for business or organizational needs, goals and objectives, and can assess the value of information technology investments in terms of the returns they bring and the opportunities they enable.

The Open Group (www.opengroup.org) is a consortium whose mission is to "work toward enabling access to integrated information within and between enterprises based on open standards and global interoperability. Recognizing the industry demand for experienced IT architects, the Open Group launched the first independent, comprehensive *IT Architect Certification Program*. The program defines global standards for measuring the skills and experience of IT architects, and for the operation of IT architecture practices within enterprises."[10]

The Open Group IT Architect Certification (ITAC) program was developed in response to a variety of emerging trends: escalating recognition of the significant business impact of architectural decisions not only to ensure return on investment but to deliver real business value, even to drive revenues; increasing acceptance, adoption, development, and convergence in the industry on the definition of an IT architect; globalization demanding that worldwide standards be defined to ensure quality control; and the need to distinguish those professionals who are most competent and experienced. The program offers three levels of certification:[11]

> ➤ Level 1: **Certified IT Architect**—able to perform with assistance/ supervision, with a wide range of appropriate skills, as a contributing architect

> ➤ Level 2: **Master Certified IT Architect**—able to perform independently and take responsibility for delivery of systems and solutions as lead architect

> ➤ Level 3: **Distinguished Certified IT Architect**—effects significant breadth and depth of impact on the business via one of three advanced career paths: Chief/Lead Architect, Enterprise Architect, or IT Architect Profession Leader.

The Open Group maintains a secure on-line listing of all certified IT architects.

Forge New Partnerships

"On every project, we're working with suppliers and other manufacturers, and IT is there to help us collaborate with third parties."

—Chris Coupland, CIO, BAE Systems

When multiple development teams are involved, consisting of both internal and external members dispersed geographically, the teams can no longer view themselves as individual entities, but must instead commit to establishing strong partnerships. The focus turns to understanding what is needed (rather than negotiating the best contract), clearly defining roles and responsibilities, and intensely collaborating every step of the way as the project progresses.

A stunning example of 21st century partnerships is the outsourcing agreement between BAE Systems (the combination of British Aerospace and Marconi Electronic Systems) and Computer Sciences Corporation (CSC). In one of the longest running alliances of its kind, "The two companies have successfully grappled with the biggest challenges in any outsourcing agreement: building mutual trust over the long haul and creating an effective deal management structure. And they have kept a focus on the business even while doing some highly complex IT implementations." As a result, IT costs were reduced by 30 percent in the first 18 months of the partnership.[12]

According to Chris Coupland, CIO of BAE Systems, in 2006 BAE discovered that the contract language for service levels with its 13-year IT outsourcer, CSC, was inadequate. Coupland explains: "So we came up with what we call the Continuous Improvement Framework (CIF), which is non-contractual. The CIF covers eight to ten different areas across the business—financial performance, service performance, and administrative tasks such as assets management, billing, invoicing, proposals, etc., mundane things that can nevertheless cause a relationship to sour if not addressed. We set targets each year that both sides buy into. We sit down and say, 'That's where we got to on asset management accuracy, or project management as a discipline, or procurement cost savings last year. Where do we want to get to this year?' And we've had a lot of success in jointly meeting those targets."[13]

Building a trusting relationship comes from working closely together, slowly earning each other's trust and confidence. "Establishing shared expectations and a requirements management process involving all stakeholders will break the cycle of misunderstanding and unfulfilled expectations." Ways to accomplish this include:[14]

➤ Build a strong cross-discipline project team

➤ Build design teams at the contractor's site that reflect the architecture of the solution

➤ Ensure that decisions are made at the level where the expertise resides

➤ Use an involved executive steering committee to make project-wide decisions

➤ Recognize and take advantage of the different cultures of the team members

➤ Encourage joint learning from mistakes at every opportunity

➤ Strive to uncover the need for rework and course correction early by accurately reporting the state of the progress

➤ Insist on open and honest communications.

Set Up System Integration Teams

System integration is all about managing dependencies—and dependencies and interrelationships are what bring about complexity. With multiple development teams, integration is *the* major risk. Integration involves combining system entities, proving that the system works as specified, and confirming that the right system has been built and that the customers/ users are satisfied.[15] Recognizing that software development is riddled with complexity, establish joint integration, verification, and validation (IV&V) teams to bring together the software and hardware components, subsystems, elements, and segments to "build up" the integrated IT system. (See the description of the Vee model in Chapter 6 for more information on IV&V.)

Techniques for the integration team to consider to limit integration complexities include planning the integration of various work flows as an "upstream" activity, planning interfaces early to anticipate integration obstacles, reusing modules whenever possible, and establishing a strong platform concept that limits dependencies, simulation, and layer-based testing.[16]

Strike the Right Balance between Discipline and Agility

"As a rule, use agile methods for emerging or rapidly evolving components, and plan-driven methods for well-understood or regulated components."

—Barry Boehm and Richard Turner

As we discussed in Chapter 2, the best approach to managing a project is to use a blend of adaptive project management approaches and conventional plan-based disciplines. The trick for the complex project manager is to determine when each approach is appropriate.

According to two experts, Barry Boehm of the University of Southern California and Richard Turner of George Washington University, "Agile development methodologies promise higher customer satisfaction, lower defect rates, faster development times and a solution to rapidly changing requirements. Plan-driven approaches promise predictability, stability, and high assurance. However, both approaches have shortcomings that, if left unaddressed, can lead to project failure. The challenge is to balance the two approaches to take advantage of their strengths and compensate for their weaknesses. We believe this can be accomplished using a risk-based approach for structuring projects to incorporate both agile and disciplined approaches in proportion to a project's needs."[17]

In their paper presented at the Agile Development Conference in 2003, Boehm and Turner offered these observations drawn from their book, *Balancing Agility and Discipline: A Guide to the Perplexed*:[18]

➤ Neither method provides a silver bullet.

➤ Both methods have environments where they are most likely to succeed, where one clearly dominates the other.

➤ Future trends are toward application developments that need both agility and discipline.

➤ Some balanced methods are emerging, such as:

  › *Agile*: Crystal Orange, DSDM (Dynamic Systems Development Method), FDD (Feature Driven Development), Lean Development

  › *Disciplined*: RUP (Rational Unified Process), CMMI® (Capability Maturity Model Integrated from the Carnegie Mellon University Software Engineering Institute)

  › *Hybrid*: Boehm/Turner Risk-Based, Agile Plus.

➤ It is better to build your method up than to tailor it down. Most plan-driven methods consist of overly rigorous processes and seldom tailor well. It is better to start with the minimum and add rigor to manage risks justified by the cost/benefit analysis.

➤ Methods are important, but are not always the answer. Potential silver bullets are more likely to be found in areas dealing with people, values, communications, and expectations management.

So how do Boehm and Turner suggest determining the right balance between agility and discipline? They propose conducting a risk-based analysis of your project centered on five key project dimensions that affect method selection (effectively collapsing our *Project Complexity Model* down to five factors):

➤ Size (number of personnel)

➤ Criticality (value of loss due to defects)

➤ Personnel (skilled versus novice)

➤ Dynamism (percent requirements change per month)

➤ Culture (percent thriving on chaos versus order).

Once the analysis is complete, it may be apparent that either the agile or the disciplined methods are needed. More likely, a mixture of the two will strike the right balance, with the method adjusted according to identified risks in each dimension. As a rule, use agile methods for emerging or rapidly evolving components and plan-driven methods for well-understood or regulated components.[19]

COMPLEXITY-REDUCING DESIGN TECHNIQUES

To build systems that are driven by the customer and adapt to environmental changes, innovative design approaches are emerging, including:

➤ Limit solution component dependencies

➤ Make use of enabling solution design tools

➤ Design for people, build for change.

Limit Solution Component Dependencies

When the technical solution is complex, it is prudent to divide the development into a core system (the operative part of the system) and special components (separate from the core, adding functionality in components). Further divide the core system into extension levels, building the foundation platform first and then extending system capabilities incrementally. As the core system is developed and implemented, different technical teams work on specialized functional components. The goal is to build the specialized components with only a one-way dependency to the core system; therefore, specialized components are independent of each other and can be created in any order or even in parallel.[20]

Make Use of Enabling Solution Design Tools

When uncertainty is high (i.e., rapidly changing requirements, technology, and even the business model) and interoperability across a complex network of suppliers and customers is needed, the use of architecture tools is essential.

Architecture tools capture, organize, and link complex information about the organization and the supporting technology; they help guide decision-making and monitor design decision implementation and success. In addition, architectural tools institutionalize standards that facilitate communication, a common language, common references, and common work products and data. When designing complex systems, a number of architectural views may be created to capture information about the operations, business systems, and technologies, with documented interrelationships between the views. This allows for a keener understanding of the dependencies within the solution that must be managed.

Design for People, Build for Change

John Rymer and Connie Moore of Forrester Research present the case that our current IT systems are sadly inadequate when it comes to keeping up with evolving markets, policies, regulations, and business models. Their proposed solution is quite futuristic: IT innovators must invent the next generation of "enterprise software that adapts to the business and its work and evolve with it . . . called *Dynamic Business Applications*." As this modernization of software development takes place, it will undoubtedly change people's jobs, how we build and modify business processes, and how we design and build software-rich products and business solutions. *Designing for people* is all about customer empowerment, collaboration, and easy access to information. *Building for change* is concerned with making organizations and their business solutions flexible, agile, and adaptive.[21]

Peter Sterpe, Senior Analyst at Forrester, surmises that the changes in how we work together will be formidable, and his predictions sound quite a bit like agile and eXtreme project methods (see Part III for a description of agile and eXtreme models): "Some people's jobs will have to change. To conceive and build applications that are context-aware and process-aware, IT will need staff that is also context-aware and process-aware. Likely changes include:[22]

➤ Business analysts will finally come into their own, bridging the divide between the business and technical communities.

➤ Developers will become experts in how their business works, and they will start to work more closely with their business and architecture experts. For developers, this also means the likely end of the waterfall model (discussed in Part III) as the project cycle of choice.

➤ Business customers will have to get more intimate with both end users and the development team; in many ways, they will start to resemble product managers.

TECHNOLOGIES THAT ENABLE CHANGE

According to Forrester, "Most business applications are too inflexible to keep pace with the businesses they support. Today's applications force people to figure out how to map isolated pools of information and functions to their tasks and processes, and they force IT pros to spend too much budget to keep up with evolving markets, policies, regulations, and business models. IT's primary goal during the next five years should be to invent a new generation of enterprise software. . . . At this stage, the requirements for Dynamic Business Applications are clearer than the design practices needed to create them. But the tools are at hand, and pioneers in service-oriented architecture (SOA), business process management (BPM), and business rules—including independent software vendors (ISVs)—have begun showing us the way. The time to start on this journey is now."[23]

Solution design and development technologies that do not use the traditional feature-based approach are rapidly emerging in the IT world. Some of the key technologies are:

➤ Service-oriented architecture

➤ Business process management

➤ Web 2.0 development

➤ Unified communications.

A word of caution: According to Forrester, agility really makes a difference in the effective application of these new technologies. "The reason business process management (BPM) implementations and service-oriented architecture (SOA) are white hot is that they make businesses significantly more agile. They enable faster responses to market conditions, new regulations, and fresh competitive opportunities. Architects play a key role in leading BPM implementations, creating the practices that ensure that SOA provides strategic business value, and selecting the right SOA-enabling technologies. And even when organizations outsource SOA development, architects are central to aligning the relationship between the business and the service provider."[24]

Service-oriented Architecture

One development method that is designed to reduce system dependencies and interrelationships is service-oriented architecture (SOA). SOA is a breakthrough software design technique that calls for the development of smaller *services* (groups of software components that perform business processes). The SOA project is a type of micro project; the Web has made it easier to standardize the technical development infrastructure, thus making micro projects feasible. The services are hooked together with other services to perform larger tasks. They are loosely coupled, have an independent interface to the core systems, and are reusable.

Web services, one of the important strategies for increasing business while reducing transaction costs, are an example of SOA. This development approach represents a transformation in how businesses and IT develop business solutions. It is an effort to drive down the total cost of ownership of IT systems, thus freeing scarce resources to develop innovative IT applications and infrastructures.[25]

A few words of caution: As organizations gain experience in SOA technology, they are discovering that it can make the IT world of software application more complex. This is because you are building many different moving parts, all of which need to be understood, maintained, and managed. "SOA was supposed to make the world simple, but that is a gross misconception," says the Hackett Group's Erik Dorr. "You are really introducing far more moving parts, you are breaking things up. SOA doesn't reduce complexity, it actually allows for a higher level of complexity."[26]

Forrester researchers warn us that the implementation of SOA architecture is no trivial task, and IT enterprise architects are key to success: "In 2008, enterprise architects will find themselves at the center of a struggle to change their organizations into significantly more agile enterprises. As solution delivery morphs from traditional in-house custom development to the integration of an amalgam of components, architects will realize that they need more than a service-oriented architecture (SOA) strategy. They will need an integrated approach to mapping out the full vision for their architectures and solutions. And they will need to rapidly develop new skills, tap into new talent, and leverage new toolsets to accommodate the increasing scope of EA initiatives."[27]

Business Process Management

Business process management (BPM) is a management approach, supported by vendor tool suites, to standardize methods to align organizational processes with the needs of customers. BPM strives to promote business effectiveness by optimizing business processes, while focusing on flexibility and innovation—just the ingredients we need when building complex adaptive business solutions.

A difficult decision needs to be made about the ownership of cross-functional business processes: Someone in the organization needs to be responsible for enterprise business processes, those that cross functional boundaries. Many argue that the effort must be driven from the top, by a senior officer of the company. In many cases the CIO is emerging as the most appropriate person to get the effort going. Forrester, in contrast, suggests the formation of teams aligned with each line of business and channel that are responsible for governing processes. These governance teams consist of representatives from all areas that support customers (marketing, sales, servicing, cross-selling, retention, etc.). The goal is to build customer-centric processes and enabling technology.[28]

BPM tools implement process-focused software in a model-driven way, rather than programmers building code manually. Tulu Tanrikorur, corporate vice president, enterprise architecture, for New York Life, introduces us to business process management tool suites.

> ### TULU TANRIKORUR, NEW YORK LIFE
> ### Business Process Management Tool Suites[29]
>
> A common confusion about BPM surrounds the difference between the workflow systems of the 1990s and today's BPMs. Older, proprietary workflow systems managed document-based processes where people executed the workflow steps of the process. The next generation workflow tools, today's BPM systems, manage processes that include person-to-person work steps, system-to-system communications, or combinations of both. In addition, BPM systems include integrated features such as enhanced (and portable) process modeling, simulation, code generation, process execution, process monitoring, customizable industry-specific templates and UI components, and out-of-box integration capabilities along with support for Web-services-based integration. All of these ingredients translate to increased interest today in BPM suites because they bring businesses a higher level of flexibility for business processes while reducing risks and cost. Think of BPM suites as offering a way to build, execute, and monitor automated processes that may go across organizational boundaries—a kind of next-generation workflow.

A similar process is value-chain analysis (see Chapter 12), which is an effective technique for assessing the feasibility of enterprise-wide solution.

Web 2.0 Development

Web 2.0 is the designation for a set of principles and practices that have come on the scene since the dot-com bubble burst in the late 1990s. To be sure, there is no widely accepted single definition for Web 2.0; however, we can say that it is a set of design patterns and business models that have come into widespread use in the 21st century, using the Web as a platform.

Web 2.0 is more about customer participation than about simply publishing information. The *emergence* of Web 2.0 (no one actually designed the Web as we know it today) is a spectacular example of a complex adaptive system. Dynamic websites replaced static web pages a decade ago; today, it is the links in current Web applications that increase the adaptive nature of the Web. The rise in blogging, which drives new value chains, is an example of Web 2.0 technologies.

The power of the Web in its current form is that it harnesses the collective intelligence that is housed on relatively small sites. Tim O'Reilly, founder and CEO of O'Reilly Media, Inc., a computer book publishing company, describes the potential unleashed by Web 2.0 technology: "The Web 2.0 lesson: leverage customer-self service and algorithmic data management to reach out to the entire web, to the edges and not just the center, to the long tail and not just the head."[30]

Unified Communications

Unified communications (UC) is an emerging technology designed to improve collaboration and speed up decision-making, as well as improve customer response and enterprise agility. UC is a software platform that brings all communications technologies together into a single solution. Elizabeth Herrell, Vice President and Principal Analyst at Forrester, suggests considering the use of unified communications software.

ELIZABETH HERRELL, FORRESTER RESEARCH
Unified Communications Software[31]

Unified communications (UC) generates interest as a potentially important business tool to improve existing business processes and reduce costly business delays for time-sensitive situations. An intelligent software platform, it connects people to people and to applications directly and easily. UC also connects desktop collaboration technologies, such as presence, email, instant messaging, and Web conferencing with communication applications (e.g., telephony, audio conferencing, voice messaging, and video). Its intuitive user interface promotes adoption and usage of UC across the enterprise. To justify UC investments, organizations should evaluate UC's business benefits and IT improvements, and explain its full value—for example, how it enables faster response to critical situations, allows employees to collaborate more easily, and reduces overhead such as travel and conferencing expenses.

Most legacy business applications that are the engine of our businesses are too inflexible to keep pace with the dynamic companies they support. In addition, many new innovative products are software-rich and are dependent on complex, customer-centric IT applications for their optimal use.

Several forward-looking managerial, design, and development techniques can be used to manage projects with a high level of IT complexity and build complex adaptive business solutions (Table 17-1). Many of these technologies are still immature, but are emerging in the IT industry as recognition grows that we need radical new methods and tools to build 21st century products and business solutions that will stand the test of time. We suggest:

- *Expert unconventional management approaches:* maintaining a fierce customer focus, fostering edge-of-chaos management, adopting a last-responsible-moment decision-making process, structuring the work into micro projects, establishing communities of practice and encouraging diversity of thought, recruiting and developing professional IT systems architects, forging new vendor and contractor partnerships, and forming integration teams.

- *Innovative design approaches:* limiting solution component dependencies, using solution design tools, and adopting a practice of designing for people but building for change.
- *New design and development technologies:* using the service-oriented architecture approach, adopting business process management principles and tool suites, pursuing Web 2.0 development practices, and using unified communication software.

Managing Projects with a High Level of IT Complexity	
Complexities	**Management Approaches**
Technical • Collection of systems functioning together to achieve a common mission • Integration issues • Unproven technology **Managerial** • Multiple contractors • Large and diverse project team • Central master plan with separate plans for subprojects • Highly visible and sensitive to political, environmental, and social issues **Agility** • Intelligent • Adaptive • Innovative • Easily changed	**Adaptive Management Techniques** • Build solutions that empower customers • Establish "skunk works" teams • Exploit the advantages of edge-of-chaos management • Introduce a last-responsible-moment decision-making process • Structure the effort into micro projects • Create communities of practice and diversity of thought • Ensure your IT architect is seasoned • Forge new partnerships • Set up integration teams • Strike the right balance between discipline and agility **Complexity-Reducing Design Techniques** • Limit solution component dependencies • Make use of enabling solution design tools • Design for people, build for change **Technologies that Enable Change** • Service-oriented architecture • Business process management • Web 2.0 development • Unified communications

TABLE 17-1. Approaches for Managing Projects with a High Level of IT Complexity

NOTES

1. The Royal Academy of Engineering, "The Challenges of Complex IT Projects" (April 2004). Online at http://www.raeng.org.uk/news/publications/list/reports/Complex_IT_Projects.pdf (accessed March 2008).

2. Elana Varon, "2007 CIO 100 Winners: How IT Can Harness the Power of Innovation" CIO. Online at http://www.cio.com/article/127400 (accessed February 2008).

3. Jim Highsmith, *Agile Project Management: Creating Innovative Products* (Boston, MA: Addison-Wesley, 2004), 6.

4. Katherine Walsh, "IT Innovations That Generate Revenue and Get You More Customers" (August 2007). Online at http://www.cio.com/article/print/127651 (accessed March 2008).

5. Elana Varon, "2007 CIO 100 Winners: How IT Can Harness the Power of Innovation" CIO. Online at http://www.cio.com/article/127400 (accessed February 2008).

6. Mary Poppendieck and Tom Poppendieck, *Lean Software Development: An Agile Toolkit* (Boston MA: Addison-Wesley, 2003).

7. James H. Johnson, "Micro Projects Cause Constant Change," The Standish Group International, Inc. (2001). Online at http://agilealliance.com/system/article/file/1053/file.pdf (accessed March 2008).

8. Linda J. Vandergriff, "Complex Venture Acquisition," Complexity Conference White Paper (2006), 9–14.

9. Ed Tittel, "IT Architects: Blueprint for a Future Career," *Certification Magazine* (2005). Online at http://www.certmag.com/articles/templates/CM_gen_Article_template. asp?articleid=1406&zoneid=225 (accessed March 2008.)

10. The Open Group. Online at http://www.opengroup.org/overview/ and http://www.opengroup .org/itac/ (accessed March 2008).

11. Ibid.

12. CSC World, *CSC and BAE: An Enduring Partnership,* 2006. Online at http://www.csc.com/ cscworld/072006/fa/fa001.shtml (accessed March 2008).

13. Ibid.

14. Birgit Seeger et al., "Tackling Complexities of In-car Embedded Systems, Viewpoint on Complexity," PA Consulting Services Limited (2005). Online at http://www.paconsulting.com/ insights/managing_complex_projects/ (accessed February 2008).

15. Hal Mooz, Kevin Forsberg, and Howard Cotterman, *Communicating Project Management* (Hoboken, NJ: John Wiley & Sons, 2003), 202.

16. Birgit Seeger et al., "Tackling Complexities of In-car Embedded Systems, Viewpoint on Complexity," PA Consulting Services Limited (2005). Online at http://www.paconsulting.com/ insights/managing_complex_projects/ (accessed February 2008).

17. Barry Boehm and Richard Turner, "Observations on Balancing Discipline and Agility," Agile Development Conference (2003).

18. Ibid.

19. Richard Turner, "Using CMMI® to Balance Agile and Plan-Driven Methods," CMMI® Technology Conference Proceeding (2003). Online at http://www.dtic.mil/ndia/2003CMMI/Turner .ppt#311,18,High Maturity

20. M. Lippert et al., "XP in Complex Project Settings: Some Extensions," Informatik/Informatique, Schweizerischer Verband der Informatikorganisationen (April 2002).

21. John Rymer and Connie Moore, "The Principles of 'Design For People, Build For Change' Will Anchor A New Generation of Business Applications," The Dynamic Business Applications Imperative (2007). Online at http://www.forrester.com/Research/Document/Excerpt/0,7211,41397,00.html (accessed March 2008).

22. Peter Sterpe, "Application Development and Program Management First Look," Forrester Research (November 2007). Online at http://www.forrester.com/FirstLook/Print/Vertical/Issue/0,,940,00.html (accessed March 2008).

23. John Rymer and Connie Moore, "The Principles of 'Design for People, Build For Change' Will Anchor a New Generation of Business Applications," The Dynamic Business Applications Imperative (2007). Online at http://www.forrester.com/Research/Document/Excerpt/0,7211,41397,00.html (accessed March 2008).

24. Larry Fulton, "Defining SOA Service Life-Cycle Management: Understanding a Core SOA Governance Process" (2008). Online at http://www.forrester.com/Research/Document/Excerpt/0,7211,43723,00.html (accessed March 2008).

25. Mark Frederick Davis, "SOA: Providing Flexibility for the Health and Science Industry" (July 2006). Online at http://h20245.www2.hpt.com/publicsector/downloads/Technology_Davis_VB.pdf (accessed September 2007).

26. Dan Briody, "Making IT Complexity Work for You" (September 2007). Online at http://www.cioinsight.com/c/a/Trends/Making-IT-Complexity-Work-for-You/2/ (accessed March 2008).

27. Larry Fulton et al., "Five Trends That Will Shape the EA Profession in 2008" (2007). Online at http://www.forrester.com/Research/Document/0,7211,43457,00.html (accessed March 2008).

28. Mary Pilecki, "Organizational Silos: Can't Live With Them and Can't Live Without Them" (2007). Online at http://www.myforrester.net/KathleenHass8151?elqPURLPage=6&elq=6279E782806D4BF1A58343B6DEAA1DBC (accessed March 2008.)

29. Tulu Tanrikorus, "Business Process Management 101: The Basics of BPM and How to Choose the Right Suite" (2007). Online at http://www.intelligententerprise.com/showArticle.jhtml?articleID=199204260 (accessed March 2008).

30. Tim O'Reilly, "What Is Web 2.0," (2005). Online at http://www.oreillynet.com/pub/a/oreilly/tim/news/2005/09/30/what-is-web-20.html?page=2 (accessed March 2008).

31. Elizabeth Herrell, "How To Evaluate Business Value For Unified Communications: Unified Communications Support Multiple Business Process Improvements" (December 2007). Online at http://www.forrester.com/Research/Document/Excerpt/0,7211,42895,00.html (accessed February 2008).

CONCLUSION TO PART IV

Complex project management is sensible chaos—striking the right balance between plans (static) and process (dynamic). We recommend using some conventional project management techniques along with some complexity thinking techniques that are "on the edge of chaos" to manage changes and uncertainties and to foster creativity and innovation.

We encourage project leaders to use the various elements of our *Project Complexity Model* during the major planning and milestone stages of a project to make informed decisions about how to manage the complexities associated with:

➤ Large, long-duration projects

➤ Large, dispersed, culturally diverse project teams

➤ Urgent projects with an aggressive scope and schedule

➤ Ambiguous business problems, opportunities, or solutions

➤ Poorly understood, volatile requirements

➤ Highly visible strategic projects that are politically sensitive

➤ Large-scale transformation initiatives

➤ Risks involved when managing projects with significant external constraints and dependencies

➤ Projects involving a high level of IT complexity.

Epilogue

As the project management discipline matures, we are coming to the realization that meeting project performance goals on time, on budget, and with a full scope of features and functions is not enough. Projects are funded to bring about positive change in organizations, leading to business benefits that are reflected in the bottom line. These business benefits may take the form of increased market share, higher levels of customer satisfaction leading to increased customer loyalty, or commercial breakthroughs that leap us ahead of the competition, to name a few.

In his research, Jim Collins discovered that leaders of great organizations strive not just for short-term goals but for enduring greatness through a paradoxical blend of personal humility and professional will. This quest is different from the vigorous pursuit of a clear and compelling vision—it is about *leaving a legacy*.[1] Complex project managers should likewise ponder what legacy they want to leave as a result of their projects. Mike Aucoin contends that "the underlying objective of any project is to put smiles on the faces and pride in the hearts of all who are involved. We want the project to elicit positive emotions in all those touched by it, and we want these positive emotions to linger long after the project is closed. This is the ultimate critical success factor for a project. This is the legacy we aspire to leave when we complete a project."[2]

Aucoin goes on to state that the perception of a product long after it is introduced is one indication of a project's legacy. If the product is highly regarded, it follows that the project will be as well, along with all those people who were associated with the project. It is imperative that the right product be delivered for a project to be considered a success. However, the right product is often difficult to determine at the beginning of a complex project. The team must be allowed to work *on the edge of chaos* for that enduring product to emerge.

As you strive to become a strong leader of complex projects, keep in mind that conventional project management techniques are based on decomposing work into simple, easily managed components. Yet sometimes, the most creative solutions emerge from teams operating on the edge of chaos. The trick is to know when to apply conventional project management techniques and when to live on the edge. Through complexity thinking, project leaders can learn to diagnose a project's complexity dimensions and then to apply appropriate management techniques.

NOTES

1. Jim Collins, *Good to Great* (New York: HarperCollins Publishers, Inc., 2001), 17–40.
2. B. Michael Aucoin, *Right-Brain Project Management: A Complementary Approach* (Vienna, VA: Management Concepts, 2007), 270.

Bibliography

Aucoin, B. Michael. 2007. *Right-Brain Project Management: A Complementary Approach.* Vienna, VA: Management Concepts.

Augustine, Sanjiv. 2005. *Managing Agile Projects.* Upper Saddle River, NJ: Prentice Hall Professional Technical Reference.

Collins, Jim. 2001. *Good to Great: Why Some Companies Make the Leap...and Others Don't.* New York: HarperCollins Publishers.

DeCarlo, Doug. 2004. *eXtreme Project Management: Using Leadership, Principles, and Tools to Deliver Value in the Face of Volatility.* San Francisco: Jossey-Bass.

Frame, J. Davidson. 2002. *The New Project Management: Tools for an Age of Rapid Change, Complexity, and Other Business Realities.* San Francisco: Jossey-Bass.

Garrett, Gregory A. 2004. *Managing Complex Outsourced Projects.* Chicago: CCH Incorporated.

Hadden, Rita Chao. 2003. *Leading Culture Change in Your Software Organization.* Vienna, VA: Management Concepts.

Hass, Kathleen B. 2008. *The Business Analyst as Strategist: Translating Business Strategies into Valuable Solutions.* Vienna, VA: Management Concepts.

Highsmith, Jim. 2004. *Agile Project Management: Creating Innovative Products.* Boston: Addison-Wesley.

Hillson, David, and Peter Simon. 2007. *Practical Project Risk Management: The ATOM Methodology.* Vienna, VA: Management Concepts.

Hillson, David, and Peter Simon. 2007. *Practical Project Risk Management: The ATOM Methodology.* Vienna, VA: Management Concepts.

Irwin, Brian. 2008. *Managing Politics and Conflict in Projects.* Vienna, VA: Management Concepts.

Johnson, Jim. 2006. *My Life is Failure: 100 Things You Should Know to be a Successful Project Leader.* West Yarmouth, MA: The Standish Group International.

Jones, Capers. 1996. *Applied Software Measurements: Assuring Productivity and Quality.* New York: McGraw-Hill.

Katzenbach, Jon R., and Douglas K. Smith. 1993. *The Wisdom of Teams.* Boston: Harvard Business School Press.

Kolb, David C. 1999. *Team Leadership.* Durango, CO: Lore International Institute.

Kotter, John P. 1996. *Leading Change.* Boston: Harvard Business School Press.

Kotter, John P. 2002. *The Heart of Change.* Boston: Harvard Business School Press.

Lewin, Roger, and Birute Regine. 1992. "On the Edge in the World of Business," afterword to *Complexity: Life at the Edge of Chaos* by Roger Lewin. Chicago: University of Chicago Press.

Lissack, Michael R., and Johan Roos. 2002. *The Next Common Sense: The e-Manager's Guide to Mastering Complexity.* London, UK: Nicholas Brealey Publishing.

Mooz, Hal, Kevin Forsberg, and Howard Cotterman. 2003. *Communicating Project Management*. Hoboken, NJ: John Wiley & Sons.

Morris, Peter W. G. 1998. *Key Issues in Project Leadership: Project Management Handbook*. San Francisco: Jossey-Bass.

Morris, Peter W. G., and Jeffrey K. Pinto. 2004. *The Wiley Guide to Managing Projects*. Hoboken, NJ: John Wiley & Sons.

Poppendieck, Mary, and Tom Poppendieck. 2003. *Lean Software Development: An Agile Toolkit*. Boston MA: Addison-Wesley.

Porter, M. E., 1985. *Competitive Advantage*. New York: Free Press.

Project Management Institute. 2004. *A Guide to the Project Management Body of Knowledge*, Third Edition. Newtown Square, PA: Project Management Institute.

Shenhar, Aaron, and Dov Dvir. 2007. *Reinventing Project Management: The Diamond Approach to Successful Growth and Innovation*. Boston: Harvard Business School Press.

Virine, Lev, and Michael Trumper. 2008. *Project Decisions: The Art and Science*. Vienna, VA: Management Concepts.

Waldrop, M. Mitchell. 1992. *The Emerging Science at the Edge of Order and Chaos*. New York: Simon & Schuster.

Williams, Terry. 2002. *Modelling Complex Projects*. West Sussex, UK: John Wiley & Sons, Ltd.

Wysocki, Robert K. 2007. *Effective Project Management, Traditional, Adaptive, Extreme,* Fourth Edition. Indianapolis, IN: Wiley Publishing, Inc.

Zook, Chris. 2007. *Unstoppable: Finding Hidden Assets to Renew the Core and Fuel Profitable Growth*. Boston: Harvard Business School Press.

Index

The Business Analysis Essential Library Series

The *Business Analysis Essential Library* is a series of practical guides that provide insight into the distinct areas of business analysis. This series provides those in the profession with the practical tools and techniques needed to operate effectively. The manuals clarify this emerging role, present contemporary business analysis practices, and explain the practical application of those practices.

Professionalizing Business Analysis: Breaking the Cycle of Challenged Projects
Kathleen B. Hass, PMP
ISBN 978-1-56726-208-7 ■ Product Code B087

Getting It Right: Business Requirement Analysis Tools and Techniques
Kathleen B. Hass, PMP, Don J. Wessels, PMP, and Kevin Brennan, PMP
ISBN 978-1-56726-211-7 ■ Product Code B117

Unearthing Business Requirements: Elicitation Tools and Techniques
Rosemary Hossenlopp, PMP, and Kathleen B. Hass, PMP
ISBN 978-1-56726-210-0 ■ Product Code B100

The Art and Power of Facilitation: Running Powerful Meetings
Alice Zavala, PMP, and Kathleen B. Hass, PMP
ISBN 978-1-56726-212-4 ■ Product Code B124

The Business Analyst as Strategist: Translating Business Strategies into Valuable Solutions
Kathleen B. Hass, PMP
ISBN 978-1-56726-209-4 ■ Product Code B094

From Analyst to Leader: Elevating the Role of the Business Analyst
Kathleen B. Hass, PMP, Richard Vander Horst, PMP, Kimi Ziemski, PMP, and Lori Lindbergh, PMP
ISBN 978-1-56726-213-1 ■ Product Code B131